WORKING WITH ROBOTS

WORKING WITH ROBOTS

HOW AI IS REDEFINING
THE WORKFORCE OF THE FUTURE

RON COHEN

NEW DEGREE PRESS

WORKING WITH ROBOTS

How AI Is Redefining The Workforce Of The Future

ISBN   978-1-64137-357-9   *Paperback*

           978-1-64137-694-5   *Ebook*

For my little daughter Netta,

May your life be filled with beautiful stories.

CONTENTS

INTRODUCTION

———

A letter came in the mail. James knew it would be coming, he had been dreading it for the past two years.

But on July 10, 2018, it arrived.

It said the following: "Dear James Dickson, congratulations on your recent graduation. You owe $148,210 for your student loan to fund your degree of Political Science. Your first payment is due on August 15, 2018, and your final payment is due July 15, 2034."

Gulp.

"I thought I had done everything right", says Dickson. "I went to school, earned a degree from a prestigious university, worked hard, went to all the networking events. So why I was forced to move back to my parents disheartened and jobless?"

James graduated with a degree in Political Science from Columbia University in New York.

"I didn't have the skills employers were looking for and couldn't find anyone willing to take a risk on me. I remember sitting around in my parent's home feeling like a loser, unsure of what I should do next, and one question didn't stop bothering me — was it all worth it?"

Think about it for a second, education is the only sector where one pays the fees, but doesn't even raise an issue for not delivering on the promise of being educated, only because in the end one gets a diploma. That's exactly like going to a restaurant, ordering a burger, getting a hot dog instead, but you're fine with it because you're going to get a receipt for the burger in the end.

Maybe it's time that students will demand more than just a certificate or diploma with the name of the college, but a real knowledge and understanding of what they're paying for.

"After discovering that I didn't have the skills employers are looking for, I was really devastated.

Turns out all of those studies were a waste of time and money. I was on the verge of giving up, but after discovering that employers struggle to find programmers, an idea sparked," recall James. "I decided to learn to program. While I was never really a "numbers guy", I bought programming books, took online courses, and also found some mentors that helped me fill in the gaps with skills and simple tricks."

"Everything changed. I almost went into shock when these newfound skills awarded me with my first job... as a software engineer!"

"When I saw my first paycheck, I couldn't help but smile and think... How fast life can change!

* * *

IT'S TIME FOR A CHANGE

The conventional path to success in the United States has looked the same for many generations.

Graduate from high school. Go to college. Earn a degree. Get a good job. Live happily ever after.

What has changed?

First, college education become too "expansive." An estimated 45 million Americans have student loans, contributing to an overall national student debt of $1.6 trillion[1]. It's time for families and future students to take a step back and seriously rethink whether that's the best option.

Second, rapid technological change, combined with anachronistic academic institutions, have made our traditional higher-education system an increasingly risky path. Colleges are not linked to future jobs and aren't teaching future skills.

I was compelled to write his book to help young people like James discover how artificial intelligence is disrupting the way we work and its implications for the future.

This is NOT a "don't go to college" book. Colleges and universities are still the best and most direct path to a good career that pays well. But if you're a student today, or about to become one, you must take ownership and responsibility of your education. If you aren't creating and owning your own trade, you're going to be passed by others.

But this book is not only for students, a lot of people are concerned about the future of work and have no idea what skills

---

1   Christopher Ingraham, "7 ways $1.6 trillion in student loan debt affects the U.S. economy", *The Washington Post*, June 25, 2019

to study or master. Nobody wants to waste time and money acquiring skills that won't be of use in the future.

We will gradually reach a period where some human skills will not be needed. Competing against robots is already a lost battle for humans. Better and cheaper robots will be able to do most of our routine tasks that require little or no creativity.

Your employer expects you to know a lot more than just what you studied at school. A degree is no longer sufficient to be indispensable at work. But you can do something about it. You have to be more accountable and responsible for your future career and develop a lifelong learning strategy.

My hope is that by reading this book, you'll understand the impact that AI and the Fourth Industrial Revolution will have on the future of work, and by knowing that, you'll understand what actions you need to take and how to master the skills that will help you adapt to the new reality.

* * *

THE ROBOTS ARE COMING

Sometime in the next five years, you're going to drive through a fast food restaurant, you'll hit a couple of buttons on a touch screen, and a window will open up and hand you your sandwich. There will be no people in there—only machines. According to a McKinsey Workforce Transition report, by 2030, as many as one-third of American jobs may disappear because of automation.[2]

But what about the highly-skilled workers, those who went to college, acquired knowledge and built their expertise? Should they be concerned as well? The short answer is yes. According to Brooking institutions, Artificial Intelligence (AI) should cause skilled and knowledgeable workers to worry too.[3]

Here's the paradox, it's really hard for computers to replicate simple tasks such as: gardening, cooking, or cutting someone's hair.

On the other hand, machines can learn how to diagnose diseases (doctors), grade essays (teachers), analyze massive amounts of data, and generate insights rapidly and accurately (consultants/accountants).

According to IEEE, the technology trade group, driverless cars are forecast to make up 75 percent of all traffic by 2040.[4] Imagine how many people will be unemployed in just the

---

2   "Jobs Lost, Jobs Gained: What The Future Of Work Will Mean For Jobs, Skills, And Wages". 2019. Mckinsey & Company.
3   Henry-Nickie, Makada. 2019. "AI Should Worry Skilled Knowledge Workers Too". Brookings
4   "Self-Driving Cars Will Take Over By 2040". 2019. Forbes.Com.

transportation industry (transformation of all the infrastructure around the job, from training to petrol stations).

Nevertheless, it's not all bad news. While we can't fight innovation or disruption, we can change with time to be relevant when the future is here. If you don't want a machine to retire you earlier than you have planned, then you should be mastering the right skills.

To adequately prepare, leaders and their employees need to focus on three things: an open mind-set, lifelong learning, and acquiring new skills. The future of work will be won by those who shift their mind-sets through learning and training.

* * *

RESKILLING AND UPSKILLING

Most conversations about the "future of work" focus on how new technologies, such as artificial intelligence, will dramatically reshape modern industries. But very few answer the question of what the earth's 7.4 billion humans should be doing now to prepare for an unpredictable future.

As it turns out, the future of work conversation is inherently a future of education conversation.

If the hallmark of twentieth century learning was access to a college education, the twenty-first century will emphasize frameworks that support lifelong learning. Education will no longer be a linear process with the endpoint of a single diploma, but a continuous and fluid process that should help us adapt to changing technological, economic, and social conditions.

As the technologies of the Fourth Industrial Revolution create new pressures on labor markets, education reform, lifelong learning, and reskilling initiatives will be key to ensuring both that individuals have access to economic opportunity by remaining competitive in the new world of work, and that businesses have access to the talent they need for the jobs of the future.

RE-skill - "reskill" essentially means to learn new skills so that you can do a different job. Reskilling can be undertaken by employers by launching proactive initiatives to determine what skills will be needed in the coming years and then comparing that to the skill set of the workforce. Reskilling can also be undertaken by individuals. Individuals can recognize that their skill sets may be dated and can opt to find ways to gain new skills on their own. This may be accomplished through participating in employer-sponsored programs, going back to school, attending conferences or seminars for additional certifications or skills, or using online programs to gain new skills.

One example for a reskilling program is the "Federal Cybersecurity Reskilling Academy pilot program." At the end of 2018, the White House launched its first program to retrain federal employees for careers in government cybersecurity. The program, run by the Education Department and CIO Council's Workforce Committee, aims to address the "critical shortage" of trained cyber talent facing the federal government. The Academy will provide feds with nontechnical backgrounds the hands-on training needed to qualify as cyber defense analysts. Those who complete the program are expected to assume positions within the government IT workforce.[5]

UP-skill - "upskill" is to teach someone additional skills, especially as an alternative to redundancy. It takes place when companies invest in training programs that help employees develop new abilities and minimize skill gaps.

"Upskilling 2025", is Amazon's plan to retrain 100,000 of its US employees by 2025. Amazon will spend $700 million over the next six years to help retrain a third of its US workforce to adapt to an economy increasingly disrupted by automation and new technology. [6]

---

5   "Want To Be A Federal Cyber Pro? This Program Will Train You". 2019. Govloop.

6   Jordan Valinsky, CNN Business. 2019. "Amazon Plans To Retrain 100,000 Employees". CNN.

Workers could use the training to transfer between positions that, without the training, they might not have been qualified for. For example, warehouse workers in fulfillment centers could be trained for technical roles in IT and nontechnical workers could be retrained as software engineers, even if they have limited technical backgrounds. "Through its Upskilling 2025 pledge, Amazon is focused on creating pathways to careers in areas that will continue growing in years to come, including healthcare, machine learning, manufacturing, robotics, computer science, cloud computing, and more," the company said in a statement.

Amazon's announcement demonstrates an understanding that the private sector must take some responsibility for the requisite upskilling and retraining. It's also a reminder that the future of work is well underway, and the jobs of tomorrow will require at least some competency in the STEM fields.

For example, ten years ago, a young individual might have secured a job at an Amazon shipping facility based on physical skills alone or in Human Resources (HR) with a simple undergraduate degree. Today, those same jobs require understanding how to work with a robot to move around packages efficiently or use AI to sift through résumés.

The reality is that we shouldn't expect an overnight shift— it won't be sudden, but it will be a dramatic shift over the coming decade. If AI and automation are the new offshoring, we need to prepare students of today for the jobs of tomorrow, while also helping today's workforce reskill and upskill to meet changing requirements. Both are Herculean tasks that require closing the gap between education and industry, as well as developing a stronger framework for credentialing in a highly fractured education landscape.

Change is coming.

Are you ready?

CHAPTER 1

THE FUTURE OF WORK IN THE DIGITAL AGE

—

- The Fourth Industrial Revolution

- Redefining work, workforces, and workplaces

- Digital Proficiency: New Talent or New Contexts?

THE FOURTH INDUSTRIAL REVOLUTION

A technological revolution is a period in which one or more technologies is replaced by another technology in a short amount of time. It is an era of accelerated technological progress characterized by new innovations whose rapid application and diffusion cause an abrupt change in society.

The Fourth Industrial Revolution describes the exponential changes to the way we live, work, and relate to one another due to the adoption of cyber-physical systems, the Internet of Things and the Internet of Systems. As we implement smart technologies in our factories and workplaces, connected machines will interact, visualize the entire production chain, and make decisions autonomously. This revolution is expected to impact all disciplines, industries, and economies.

Like the First Industrial Revolution's steam-powered factories, the Second Industrial Revolution's application of science to mass production and manufacturing, and the Third Industrial Revolution's start into digitization, the Fourth Industrial Revolution's technologies, such as artificial intelligence, genome editing, augmented reality, robotics, and 3-D printing, are rapidly changing the way humans create, exchange, and distribute value. As occurred in the previous revolutions, this will profoundly transform institutions, industries, and individuals. [7]

---

7 "The Fourth Industrial Revolution | Special Feature". 2019. Encyclopedia Britannica.

Figure-1: The Industrial Revolutions

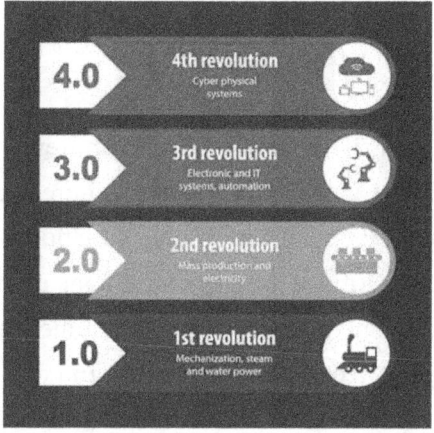

Source: https://www.britannica.com/topic/The-Fourth-Industrial-Revolution-2119734

In his book, *The Fourth Industrial Revolution*, Professor Klaus Schwab, founder and executive chairman of the World Economic Forum, describes the enormous potential for the technologies of the Fourth Industrial Revolution, as well as the possible risks. He said, "The changes are so profound that, from the perspective of human history, there has never been a time of greater promise or potential peril. My concern, however, is that decision-makers are too often caught in traditional, linear (and non-disruptive) thinking or too absorbed by immediate concerns to think strategically about the forces of disruption and innovation shaping our future."[8]

---

8 *Klaus Schwab, The Fourth Industrial Revolution, January 3,*

This revolution is not just happening to us - we are not its victims - but rather we have the opportunity and even responsibility to give it structure and purpose.

As economists Erik Brynjolfsson and Andrew McAfee have pointed out, this revolution could yield greater inequality, particularly in its potential to disrupt labor markets. "As automation substitutes for labor across the entire economy, the net displacement of workers by machines might exacerbate the gap between returns to capital and returns to labor. On the other hand, it is also possible that the displacement of workers by technology will, in aggregate, result in a net increase in safe and rewarding jobs." [9]

All previous industrial revolutions have had both positive and negative impacts on different stakeholders. Nations have become wealthier, and technologies have helped pull entire societies out of poverty, but the inability to fairly distribute the resulting benefits or anticipate externalities has resulted in global challenges.

The Fourth Industrial Revolution is, therefore, not a prediction of the future, but a call to action. It is a vision for developing, diffusing, and governing technologies in ways that foster a more empowering, collaborative, and sustainable

---

9   *"The Fourth Industrial Revolution: What It Means And How To Respond". 2019. World Economic Forum.*

foundation for social and economic development, built around shared values of the common good, human dignity, and intergenerational stewardship. Realizing this vision will be the core challenge and great responsibility of the next fifty years.

REDEFINING WORK, WORKFORCES, AND WORKPLACES

Maybe in your particular future of work, you imagine factories full of robots, automating commonplace tasks, while human beings orchestrate the work's ultimate goals and intent. Perhaps, you think of the working population's shifting demographics, with the workforce growing older in developed nations, while emerging economies struggle to assimilate record numbers of young workers. Or, you may envision a global Gig Economy (a general workforce environment in which short-term engagements, temporary contracts, and independent contracting is commonplace) in which most individuals work for themselves, online or in person—to a variety of employers on their own time and terms.

The future of work could involve all of these scenarios and more. The outlines of the picture are already emerging. Indeed, it may be misleading to explore all this under the heading of "the future of work" which suggests that the changes are not yet here and will occur in an indeterminate number of years. The truth is that many of these changes are already playing out.

In a new model, Deloitte examines the components that collectively constitute "the future of work." Deloitte's research identified three forces that are shaping the nature of future work and the future workforce:

1. *Technology*: Advances in technology have created entirely new ways of getting work done that are, in some cases, upending the way we use and think about our tools and how people and machines can complement and substitute for one another (e.g., robotics, artificial intelligence, sensors, and data).

2. *Demographics*: Demographic changes are shifting the composition of the global workforce. Much of the world is challenged by longer lifespans, with populations becoming both older and younger, as well as more diverse. Even more challenging, the younger generations will be increasingly concentrated in developing economies, while the developed economies (and China) get even older.

3. *"The power of pull"*: Large thanks to digital technologies and long-term public policy shifts, individuals and institutions can exert greater "pull"—the ability to find and access people and resources when and as needed—than ever before. Institutions and prospective workers alike now have access

to global talent markets, enabled by networks and platforms opening up new possibilities for the way each interacts with the other. The demand for these platforms will likely be enhanced by increasing customer power and accessibility of productive tools and machines, opening up opportunities for more creative work to be done in smaller enterprises and by entrepreneurial ventures.[10]

These three driving forces are having two significant effects on work and the workforce.

First, technology is transforming the nature of work and forcing organizations to redesign most jobs. One result, the research anticipates, will be the reconfiguration of jobs to leverage uniquely human skills: empathy, social and emotional intelligence, the ability to set context and define business problems. Another, due to the accelerating rate of technological change, will be the need for individuals to continually learn new skills to remain employable.

Second, the relationship between employer and worker is shifting. Where once physical proximity was required for people to get work done, the advent of digital communication, collaboration platforms, and digital reality technologies, along with societal and marketplace changes, have allowed for and created the

---

10   *"Preparing Tomorrow'S Workforce For The Fourth Industrial Revolution". 2019.*

opportunity for more distributed teams. Organizations are now able to orchestrate a range of options as they reimagine workplaces, from the more traditional collocated workplaces to those that are completely distributed and dependent on virtual interactions. Organizations now have a broad continuum of options for finding workers, from hiring traditional full-time employees to availing themselves of managed services and outsourcing, independent contractors, gig workers, and crowdsourcing. [11]

Figure-2: Spectrum of worker types and work arrangements

FIGURE 2

The talent market covers a spectrum of worker types and work arrangements

Traditional — Best for function-specific work

Open — Best for task-specific work

Open talent continuum

Organization's employees | Joint venture employees | Managed service providers | Contractors | Gig workers | Crowd

Source: Deloitte analysis.

Deloitte Insights | deloitte.com/insights

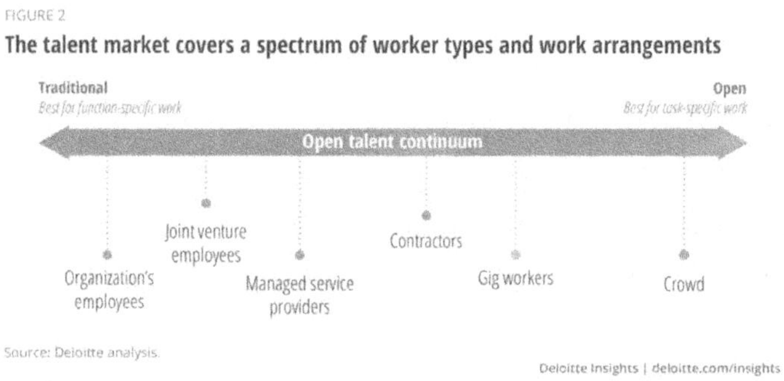

BEYOND THE EMPLOYEE LIFE CYCLE

Organizations have long thought of talent management as how to approach attracting, developing, and retaining top talent. As new, alternative work arrangements come on the scene, Deloitte anticipates that this model could shift to:

---

11 *ibid*

Access: How do you tap into capabilities and skills across your enterprise and the broader ecosystem? This includes sourcing from internal and external talent marketplaces and leveraging and mobilizing on- and off-balance sheet talent.

Curate: How do you provide employees, ecosystem talent, and teams with the broadest and most meaningful range of development? This includes work experiences that are integrated into the flow of their work, careers, and personal lives.

Engage: How do you interact with and support your workforces, business teams, and partners to

build compelling relationships? This includes multidirectional careers in, across, and outside of the enterprise; and for business leaders and teams, providing insights to improve productivity and impact while taking advantage of new ways of teaming and working.[12]

THE FUTURE IS UNPREDICTABLE

Despite these predictions on the changing workforce, it remains nearly impossible to anticipate precisely which occupations will thrive in the year to come. The parents of today's social media managers and search engine evaluators—couldn't

---

12   *"From Employee Experience To Human Experience: Putting Meaning Back Into Work". 2019.*

possibly have known those roles would exist when they were helping their children decide which subjects to study at school.

The following high-level trends can give you an idea of where to focus your attention.

Figure-3: Job families in decline and on the rise[13]

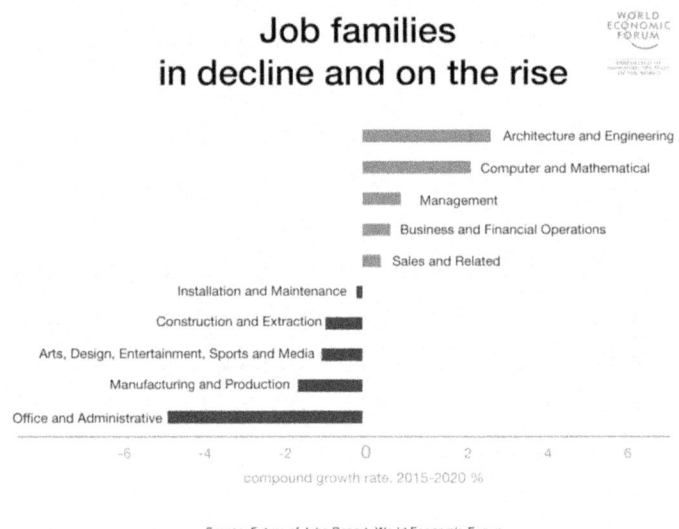

Source: Future of Jobs Report, World Economic Forum

BUSINESSES NEED TO RETHINK EVERYTHING

Forget the rigid corporate ladder. Today, the most attractive and best places to work allow free-flowing ideas and career

---

13   *"Employment Trends". 2019. The Future Of Jobs.*

paths. In the industrial age, businesses were built on strict hierarchy. Today, in the digital age, we are witnessing a major shift. As thought patterns, economic times, and digital technology evolves, the traditional work environment is growing, changing, and emerging with the times. The future of work is a lifestyle of personal preferences, personal development, and personal responsibility. The future of work means fewer hours spent onsite, locked into a cubicle, and punching a time clock tied to a rigid set of hours and rules.[14]

It means remote teams, separate but collaborative teamwork, and working around one's lifestyle.

This is evidenced by the growing number of specialized business consultants, the prevalence of freelancers, and the continued emergence of the gig economy. Today, businesses are learning to adapt to the creativity and flexibility of the modern worker and the modern workplace.

As employees learn to embrace a shared vision for the companies they represent, a new culture is being created and established. Increasing digitization, the rise of digital natives and productivity pressures are causing businesses to rethink everything.

---

14   *"The Future Of Work Is Creative, Flexible, And Human".*
      2019. Medium.

Consider this: Airbnb, the world's largest accommodation provider, actually owns no property.

Facebook, the world's largest media company, generates no content. Or Uber, the world's largest taxi company, owns no cars.[15]

Figure-4: The Digital Disruption

Source: Digital disruption at an unprecedented speed and scale

THE FUTURE OF WORK IS CREATIVE, FLEXIBLE, AND HUMAN

"Humans have always been born with creative skills," says Dr. Gavin Suss, Dean—School of Design and Innovation, The College of Management Academic Studies. "Think about it, how can you explain the survival of the human

---

15 *"Disruptive Technologies And Their Impact On The Future Of Work". 2019.*

race? Throughout history, humans have been able to develop tools that will help them survive, sustain and grow against wars, diseases and natural disasters. The current period is no different, rather it's even more challenging today."

"The problem today is, that most of us live in our comfort zone. We don't really have the need to be creative, and innovation that serves as the main engine to organizational growth is the direct outcome of creative human beings."

The good news according to Suss, is that creativeness is a muscle that can be trained. "You can teach people to be more open minded, more creative, and less judgmental. To do so, higher education institutions need to adopt a different and a less anachronistic attitude." "Our economy, and essentially the human society, needs creative workers and leaders to successfully stand up to the challenges that the future will bring."

Examples of roles in the creativity sector of the near future include 3D printing fashion designer, virtual reality (VR) experience designer and augmented reality architects. These jobs will be driven by the rise of novel creative tools such as 3D printing and virtual reality, among existing digital tools.

What is notable about such roles is that at their very core, they are multidisciplinary. Many of them are examples of Science,

Technology, Engineering, Art, and Math (STEAM) skills in which the "A" stands for the arts, in its broadest definition (including liberal and fine arts along with humanities). For instance, a VR experience designer will have to combine expertise from both the arts and technology to create immersive VR worlds. Hence, it is also a strong case for bringing more STEAM learning into traditional education.[16]

Our future economy will be built on creativity and technology. The digital revolution won't render people obsolete. But it is a paradigm shift. There will be immense opportunities for people who combine creative, technical, and social skills—skills that are resilient to future automation.

When individuals work separately, then come together to create a whole, they bring increased innovation and originality to the table. New ideas are more readily introduced and embraced when creativity and imagination are allowed to flourish and thrive.

Employees feel most appreciated when they're given creative freedom and viewed as valuable resources as opposed to being seen as dispensable. The workplace of the future must adapt and learn to trust employees to manage their own time, productivity, and personal development.

---

16   Georgette Yakman, "Developing STEAM Education To Improve Students' Innovative Ability | STEAM Education". 2019. STEAM Education.

As companies define the work they need done and the projects they need completed, they create new teams and departments. The key is in understanding how those teams and departments come together to create a company-wide whole. When several freelancers, contractors, consultants, and gig economy workers are collaborating on a singular project, they become a de facto team.

Contemporary and emerging technology means these teams might work together without ever seeing each other face-to-face.

HUMANS + GIGS + ROBOTS ARE THE NEW BLENDED WORKFORCE

"The future workforce will combine private full-time workers, public freelancers, and bots", Says Infosys President Ravi Kumar.

According to Kumar, there is no question that organizations are moving from a private human capital talent pool of primarily full-time workers to one also encompassing a virtual pool of on-demand workers who are supplemented by machines automating routine tasks.

This new blended workforce is one of five emerging trends shaping the future of work:

1. *The blended workforce of humans + gigs + robots will be the new normal.* The movement from a homogenous workforce of FTE's to a heterogeneous workforce of humans on the premises, working in tandem with a virtual pool of gig talent and robots, will be the new normal.

    In this new blended workforce of Humans + Gigs+ Robots, humans will be able to work smarter because of the scale and agility of Gig workers and real time data insights provided by machines.

2. *The future of skills will move from linear to Z-shaped skills.* This notion of developing cross functional skills is not new, in fact the notion of "T" shaped skills was first described in 1991. "T" shaped individuals combine both a depth and breadth of skills possessing deep functional expertise with well-honed social skills to collaborate across disciplines. Z-shaped skills combine deep business & digital literacy with soft skills of the Five C's: Collaboration, Critical Thinking, Communications, Cultural Fluency and Change Management along with a focus on Creativity and Innovation. The forerunner of this commitment to the intersection between business, technology, and design capabilities was Steve Jobs. As Steve Jobs once said, "The Macintosh turned out so well because the people working on it were musicians, artists, poets, and historians - who also happened to be computer scientists."

3. *The secret sauce to building talent pools with Z-shaped skills requires innovative thinking in building corporate university partnerships.* As organizations recruit for Z-shaped skills, they need to move beyond recruiting just for STEM focused talent to recruiting a broader talent from liberal arts, design, and even community colleges.

4. *The democratization of technology skills will blur the lines between white collar, blue collar and new-collar jobs.* Using data is becoming democratized, and increasing the data literacy of everyone in the organization, not just the data scientists, will be the goal of the future workplace.

    As we envision the future, we see more organizations making an investment in ensuring every worker has a baseline set of digital skills. A new category of jobs known as New Collar jobs, or positions that require specific skills but not a bachelor's degree, are in high demand today.

5. *The CEO will become the Evangelist for A Growth Mindset.* As Satya Nadella, CEO of Microsoft, says, the future belongs to organizations that build a culture of "learn-it-all's, rather than know-it-all's." Building a growth mindset and commitment to continuous learning means senior leaders must become role models for learning and creativity. Those who fully commit to this will create a competitive advantage for their organizations.

DIGITAL PROFICIENCY: NEW
TALENT OR NEW CONTEXTS?

The extent of digitalization and its impact are unparalleled. According to Gartner, "87 percent

of business executives agree that digitalization is a priority for their company"[17]. They expect its impact to grow. Sixty-seven percent of those same executives believe their organizations must become significantly more digitized to remain competitive. The move toward digital, customer first business strategies, products, and services alters how organizations operate, how work gets done, and the contexts in which employees do their jobs. In other words, it creates a new digital business environment.

A digital business is enabled through talent—placing people at the heart of the business agenda. Across all industries and continents, talent attraction, talent management, and leadership development have become issues of significant global concern. Increasingly, organizations are finding it difficult to attract, hire, develop, and retain the talent they need to meet their business objectives.

The idea that digitalization is a force leading to fundamental changes in every organization and industry raises the essential question of whether the talent they need to succeed is also fundamentally different.

---

17 *"Gartner Survey Reveals That CEO Priorities Are Shifting To Embrace Digital Business". 2019. Gartner.*

SHL has identified four primary digital talent objectives they tend to share.[18]

These key objectives set the requirements for the profile of the digital talent organizations need to succeed. "We consider individuals with this profile to be "digitally proficient." Digital proficiency is the ability to engage in the behaviors (or competencies) necessary to perform well in a digital business environment."

Digital Talent Objectives	Digitalization's Impact	Key Competencies
Continuous Learning and Innovation	The rapid pace of change associated with digital business environments and transformations requires employees and leaders who can adapt, learn effectively, and innovate to drive their organizations forward.	• Learning • Adaptability • Creativity and Innovation • Strategic Thinking
Insightful Analytics	The explosion of new digital tools and the exponential growth of data and information require employees who can apply their analytical and reasoning skills to effectively use those tools and data to create insights that produce results in a wide range of contexts.	• Applying Expertise and Technology • Critical Thinking
Network Performance	The increased interdependence of work and stronger emphasis on the customer experience in digital business environments requires employees who can develop productive relationships, collaborate, and influence others to boost the performance of their colleagues and customers. That is, they deliver digital network performance	• Collaboration • Building Relationships • Influence
Execution Excellence	The pressure for sustained top line and bottom line financial growth of digital businesses requires employees and leaders who are action-oriented, decisive, pragmatic, and efficient in achieving their performance goals and objectives.	• Decision Making • Planning and Organizing • Delivering Results • Initiative

Source: SHL's Universal Competency Framework TM.

---

18 *"The SHL Talent Report". 2019. Lessaccent.Com.*

Continuous Learning and Innovation: Continuous learning and innovation is the digital talent priority borne out of the unrelenting pace of change in digital business environments. Organizations are constantly changing: 98 percent of employees report significant changes to their business in the past four years. Most of the jobs that people have and the products and services their organizations provide today will be markedly different three to four years from now. Digitally proficient employees must not only keep up with and adapt to change, but also drive change toward high levels of performance.

Insightful Analytics: The optimal use of data and information is the objective most likely to come to mind when considering what digitally-proficient employees need to achieve. It's almost a given that it should be included in any model or perspective of digital talent. For example, the World Economic Forum predicts that "by 2022, 85 percent of respondents are likely, or very likely, to have expanded their adoption of big data analytics." Many models operate with the assumption that these new tools and types of data require entirely new types of employees. Certainly, their form and nature have been, and are, rapidly evolving.

Network Performance: The digital talent objective involving network performance is probably the broadest, but also most overlooked area for success in the digital business environment. It's easily taken for granted, since nearly every job requires some interaction with other individuals, whether inside or outside an organization. However, the digital environment places even greater emphasis on leveraging relationships. Much like the services digital businesses offer, the work activities and processes of these organizations are heavily interconnected or networked. It places a premium on network-driven performance that relies on the contributions that employees make to help one another accomplish their tasks.

Execution Excellence: Execution excellence may seem to be an odd priority for digital talent. After all, in which environments and businesses would execution not be a priority? Execution ranks high in almost any organization, but it's especially difficult and important in a digital business environment.

All three of the objectives above illustrate why execution is so challenging. These environments are dynamic, ambiguous, information-rich, and interconnected. Staying focused on delivering results is critical under any of these conditions. Yet, the level of competition and need for digital businesses to continuously match or outpace their competition shows no signs of diminishing. The pressure for continuous double-digit growth levels is enormous.

HOW BUSINESSES CAN WIN THE DIGITAL TALENT WAR?

The war for digital talent had begun, this reality represents one of the biggest challenges facing companies today. The only way businesses can win this war is by understanding their digital needs and taking a different approach to their talent strategy.

Before all else, organizations must have a clear vision for how digital capabilities will improve their operational efficiency and customer value. While the needs will vary depending on market and geography, companies are generally more dependent on the collective skills of a multidisciplinary team, which also means that good teamwork is almost as important as strong technical skills.

Experience designers and engineers, scrum masters and agility coaches, product owners, full-stack architects and, increasingly, next-gen machine-learning engineers and "DevOps" engineers (the integration of development and operations) should be part of any company's tech-talent list.

While retaining, training and uncovering existing talent should be part of a good talent strategy, companies need to acquire talent to meet these growing digital needs. McKinsey lists six ways to successfully build a digital talent pool:[19]

---

19   *"The New Tech Talent You Need To Succeed In Digital".*
     2019. Mckinsey & Company.

1. Build a compelling vision by presenting an inspiring mission.

2. Make targeted 'anchor hires', who are leaders in a particular discipline to attract further talent.

3. Reimagine recruiting using non-traditional platforms and drafting top-performers within the organization to recruit their peers.

4. Create a network of digital-labor platforms, where employees share job satisfaction, company culture and lifestyle information.

5. Build an ecosystem of vendor partners, which includes traditional vendors, new partners, alliances, and crowd-sourcing.

6. "Acqui-hiring" talent by acquiring a start-up with specific needed capabilities.

* * *

Business leaders are already recognizing that technology-related talent is crucial to achieving their digital transformation goals. However, in order to win the digital talent war, they must therefore change their approach to attracting and retaining employees whose capabilities are increasingly scarce.

CHAPTER 2

THE SYMBIOTIC WORKFORCE OF THE FUTURE

- Can Machines Think?

- The AI Effect on Jobs

- Collaborative Intelligence: Humans and AI Are Joining Forces

- The Future of Collaboration

- Having a Robot as a Colleague

CAN MACHINES THINK?

When you think of artificial intelligence, your thought immediately goes to robots or anything automated. Even though you're right, what if I told you artificial intelligence is so much more than just robots?

In the first half of the twentieth century, science fiction familiarized the world with the concept of artificially intelligent robots. It began with the "heartless" Tin man from the *Wizard of Oz* and continued with the humanoid robot that impersonated Maria in *Metropolis.* By the 1950s, we had a generation of scientists, mathematicians, and philosophers with the concept of artificial intelligence (or AI) culturally assimilated in their minds.

One such person was Alan Turing, a young British polymath who explored the mathematical possibility of artificial intelligence. Turing suggested that humans use available information as well as reason to solve problems and make decisions, so why can't machines do the same thing? This was the logical framework of his 1950 paper, *Computing Machinery and Intelligence,* in which he discussed how to build intelligent machines and how to test their intelligence.[20]

What stopped Turing from getting to work right then and there? First, computers needed to fundamentally change.

---

20 *"The History Of Artificial Intelligence - Science In The News".*
2019. Science In The News.

Before 1949, computers lacked a key prerequisite for intelligence: they couldn't store commands, only execute them. In other words, computers could be told what to do, but couldn't remember what they did. Second, computing was extremely expensive. In the early 1950s, the cost of leasing a computer ran up to $200,000 a month. Only prestigious universities and big technology companies could afford to buy them.

During the next forty years, computers have been developed to store more information and become faster, cheaper, and more accessible. Machine learning algorithms also improved, and people got better at knowing which algorithm to apply to their problem. But still, the biggest challenge was the lack of computational power to do anything substantial: computers simply couldn't store enough information or process it fast enough.

During the 1990s and 2000s, many of the landmark goals of artificial intelligence had been achieved, and in 1997, reigning world chess champion and grand master, Gary Kasparov, was defeated by IBM's Deep Blue, a chess playing computer program. This highly publicized match was the first time a reigning world chess champion lost to a computer and served as a huge step towards an artificially intelligent decision-making program.

Today, artificial intelligence's progress is staggering. Efforts to advance AI concepts over the past twenty years have resulted in some truly amazing innovations. It's likely that you've interacted with some form of AI in your day-to-day activities. If you use Gmail, for example, you may enjoy the automatic email filtering feature. If you own a smartphone, you probably fill out a calendar with the help of Siri, Cortana, or Bixby. If you own a newer vehicle, perhaps you've benefited from a driver-assist feature while driving.

Sundar Pichai, Google CEO, explains it in his own words: "It is important to help people understand that they use AI today. AI is just making computers more intelligent and being able to do a wide variety of tasks and we take it for granted whenever something happens, and we adopt it. For example, today, Google can translate across many languages and people use it billions of times a day. That's because of AI."[21]

According to Pichai, artificial intelligence is going to have a bigger impact on the world than some of the most ubiquitous innovations in history. "AI is one of the most important things humanity is working on. It is more profound than, electricity or fire. AI holds the potential for some of the biggest advances we are going to see. You know whenever I see the news of a young person dying of cancer, I realize AI is going to play a role in solving that in the future, so I think we owe it to make progress." [22]

---

21 *Clifford, Catherine. 2019. "Google CEO: A.I. Is More Important Than Fire Or Electricity".*
22 *ibid*

THE AI EFFECT ON JOBS

As artificial intelligence invades more and more aspects of our lives, one of the big questions on everyone's mind is how it will affect our jobs. Will we eventually enjoy the luxury of working just a few hours a week, while bots handle all the most disagreeable chores for us? Or, will AI systems take all the good jobs, leaving human beings in a permanent underclass?

According to the World Economic Forum (WEF) report on the Future of Jobs 2018, "Machines currently handle about 29 percent of tasks across the twelve industries studied. By 2022, 42 percent of all tasks and 62 percent of data processing and search likely will be handled by machines and algorithms." [23] That's a dramatic shift over just four years, and it could have a very noticeable impact on day-to-day work activities.

McKinsey Global Institute's latest report, Jobs lost, jobs gained: Workforce transitions in a time of automation, assesses the number and types of jobs that might be created under different scenarios through 2030 and compares that to the jobs that could be lost to automation.

The report suggests that "By 2030, intelligent agents and robots could replace as much as 30 percent of the world's

---

23 *"The Future Of Jobs Report 2018". 2019. World Economic Forum.*

current human labor." [24]McKinsey reckons that, depending upon various adoption scenarios, "Automation will displace between 400 and 800 million jobs by 2030, requiring as many as 375 million people to switch job categories entirely."

Their key finding is that while there may be enough work to maintain full employment to 2030 under most scenarios, the transitions will be very challenging—matching or even exceeding the scale of shifts out of agriculture and manufacturing we have seen in the past.

HUMANITY WATCH OUT - ROBOTS ARE COMING TO TAKE YOUR JOB

The fear of robots coming for your job is one of the many challenges confronting 21st-century workers. When technology comes in, and some workers go away, there is a residual fear among those still in place at the company. It's only natural for them to ask, "Am I next? How many more days will I be employed here?"

The wise corporate leader will realize that post-technology trauma falls along two lines: (1) how to integrate the new technology into the work flow, and (2) how to cope with feelings that the new technology is somehow "the enemy." Without dealing with both, even the most automated workplace could easily have undercurrents of anxiety, if not anger.

---

24 *"JOBS LOST, JOBS GAINED: WORKFORCE TRANSITIONS IN A TIME OF AUTOMATION". 2019. Mckinsey.Com.*

"Without urgent and targeted action today, to manage the near-term transition and build a workforce with future-proof skills, governments will have to cope with ever-growing unemployment and inequality, and businesses with a shrinking consumer base," [25] said Klaus Schwab, Founder and Executive Chairman of the World Economic Forum.

THE INDUSTRIES THAT ARE MOST LIKELY TO BE TAKEN OVER BY ROBOTS

"Humans are strategic; machines are tactical" McKinsey has been studying what kind of work is most adaptable to automation. Their findings, so far, seem to conclude that the more technical the work, the more technology can accomplish it. In other words, machines skew toward tactical applications.

McKinsey noted that tasks like physical labor in a predictable environment, such as a fast-food restaurant or a factory assembly line, and basic data processing, like tracking payroll accounting, could easily be automated using the robots and software available to us now.

On the other hand, work that requires a high degree of imagination, creative analysis, and strategic thinking is harder to automate. As McKinsey put it in a recent report: "The hardest

---

25 *"Employment Trends". 2019. The Future Of Jobs.*

activities to automate with currently available technologies are those that involve managing and developing people (9 percent automation potential) or that apply expertise to decision making, planning, or creative work (18 percent)."[26]

This chart below shows the estimated average share of time spent by workers in each industry sector on tasks that could theoretically be automated using current technology, according to McKinsey's analysis.[27]

Figure-5: Share of time spent in tasks

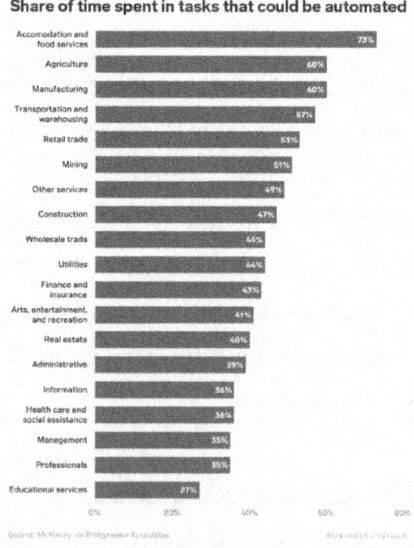

Share of time spent in tasks that could be automated

---

26   *"Where Machines Could Replace Humans--And Where They Can'T (Yet)". 2019. Mckinsey & Company.*

27   *ibid*

THE MOST AUTOMATABLE ACTIVITIES

Almost one-fifth of the time spent in US workplaces involves performing physical activities or operating machinery in a predictable environment: workers carry out specific actions in well-known settings where changes are relatively easy to anticipate. [28]Through the adaptation and adoption of currently available technologies, McKinsey estimates the technical feasibility of automating such activities at 78 percent, the highest of seven top-level categories. Since predictable physical activities figure prominently in sectors such as manufacturing, food service and accommodations, and retailing, these are the most susceptible to automation based on technical considerations alone.

McKinsey pointed out that their analysis focused on what tasks could potentially be automated using current technology, which doesn't necessarily mean that these jobs actually will end up being more heavily done by robots and software. Other economic and social concerns, like the cost of labor relative to new investment in advanced machines and the public's willingness to have robots do things like serve them food, are likely to be big factors in whether or not various jobs and tasks actually do become automated, according to the report.

---

28 *ibid*

ACTIVITIES WITH LOW TECHNICAL
POTENTIAL FOR AUTOMATION

The hardest activities to automate with currently available technologies are those that involve managing and developing people (9 percent automation potential) or that apply expertise to decision making, planning, or creative work (18 percent). These activities, often characterized as knowledge work, can be as varied as coding software, creating menus, or writing promotional materials. For now, computers do an excellent job with very well-defined activities, such as optimizing trucking routes, but humans still need to determine the proper goals, interpret results, or provide commonsense checks for solutions. The importance of human interaction is evident in two sectors that, so far, have a relatively low technical potential for automation: healthcare and education.

COUNTRIES WITH THE MOST ROBOT WORKERS

Data from the International Federation of Robotics reveals that the pace of industrial automation is accelerating across much of the developed world with seventy-four installed industrial robots per 10,000 employees globally in 2016. A year later, that increased to eighty-five across the manufacturing sector. Europe has a robot density of 106 units per 10,000 workers and that number is ninety-one and seventy-five in the Americas and Asia, respectively. China is one of the countries recording the highest growth levels in industrial automation, but no place has a robot density like South Korea.[29]

In 2017, South Korea had 710 installed industrial robots per 10,000 employees. That is mainly due to the continued installation of high-volume robots in the electronics and electric sectors. Ninety percent of Singapore's industrial robots are installed in its electronics industry and it comes second with a density of 658 per 10,000 employees. Germany and Japan are renowned for their automotive industries and they have density levels of just over 300 per 10,000 workers. Interestingly, Japan is one of the main players in industrial robotics, accounting for 56 percent of global supply. [30]

In the United States, the pace of automation is slower with a density rate of 200. China is eager to expand its level of automation in the coming years, targeting a place in the world's top ten nations for robot density by 2020. It had a density rate of twenty-five units in 2013 and that grew to ninety-seven by 2017. In 2017, China was already supplying 36 percent of the robots sold.[31]

---

29 *"These Countries Have The Most Robot Workers". 2019. World Economic Forum.*
30 *ibid*
31 *"Robot Density Rises Globally". 2019. IFR International Federation Of Robotics*

Figure-6: Countries with the highest density of robot workers

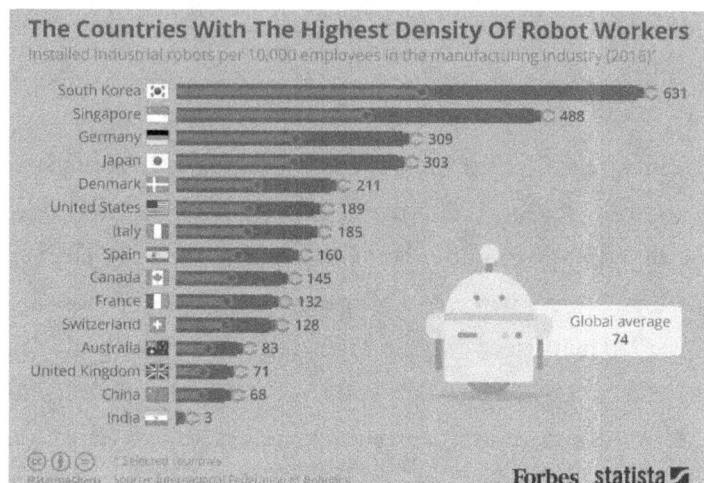

The Countries With The Highest Density Of Robot Workers
Installed industrial robots per 10,000 employees in the manufacturing industry (2016)

South Korea	631
Singapore	488
Germany	309
Japan	303
Denmark	211
United States	189
Italy	185
Spain	160
Canada	145
France	132
Switzerland	128
Australia	83
United Kingdom	71
China	68
India	3

Global average 74

Forbes statista

AI COULD GROW JOBS: INVENTING NEW
ONES, EMPOWERING EXISTING ONES

2020 will be a pivotal year in AI-related employment dynamics. Gartner predicts that "By 2020, AI will create more jobs than it eliminates."[32]

"Many significant innovations in the past have been associated with a transition period of temporary job loss, followed by recovery, then business transformation and AI will likely follow this route," says Svetlana Sicular, Research Vice President at Gartner. According to Sicular "AI will improve the productivity of many

---

32 *"Gartner Says By 2020, Artificial Intelligence Will Create More Jobs Than It Eliminates". 2019. Gartner.*

jobs, eliminating millions of middle - and low-level positions, but also creating millions more new positions of highly skilled, management and even the entry-level and low-skilled variety."[33]

Yes, layoffs are inevitable going forward, but what much of the chatter ignores is that the future will also see employment creation, including jobs that are as yet unheard of. For example, in the past century, we've seen the demise or diminishment of titles such as travel agent, switchboard operator, milkman, elevator operator, and bowling alley pinsetter. Meanwhile, new titles like app developer, social media director, and data scientist have emerged.

Take the recent "Future of Jobs in India" study, commissioned jointly by FICCI and NASSCOM with EY. The report looks at the impact of advanced technologies on five key manufacturing and services sectors in India—IT/ITeS, retail, financial services, textile and apparel, and auto—that create the bulk of jobs. A key finding was that "9 percent of India's 600 million estimated workforce would be deployed in new jobs that do not exist today, while 37 percent would be in jobs that have radically changed skill sets."[34]

That's not all, in addition to creating new jobs, AI will actually help us do our jobs better—a lot better.

---

33   *ibid*
34   *"Future of jobs in India" 2019. Ey.Com.*

The reality is, that these technologies will transform the nature of work and the workplace itself, machines will be able to carry out more of the tasks done by humans, complement the work that humans do, and even perform some tasks that go beyond what humans can do.

"Now is the time to really impact your long-term AI direction," said Sicular. "For the greatest value, focus on augmenting people with AI. Enrich people's jobs, reimagine old tasks and create new industries. Transform your culture to make it rapidly adaptable to AI-related opportunities or threats."

COLLABORATIVE INTELLIGENCE: HUMANS AND AI ARE JOINING FORCES

AI AUGMENTATION

AI Augmentation - is a combination of human and artificial intelligence, where both complement each other. The real value of automation and AI lies in augmenting the workforce; the ability to collectively make sense of the world that makes us uniquely human and separates us from the robots. "In 2021, AI augmentation will create $2.9 trillion of business value and 6.2 billion hours of worker productivity globally", [35] according to Gartner.

---

35 *"Gartner Says AI Augmentation Will Create $2.9 Trillion Of Business Value In 2021". 2019. Gartner*

That means that rather than replacing workers, AI can be a tool to help employees work better. As we've already seen in the airline business, autopilot didn't put pilots out of a job; instead it foreshadowed an increasing collaboration between human and machine on complex tasks. A call center employee, for instance, can get instant intelligence about what the caller needs and do their work faster and better. In another example, in life sciences, Accenture is using deep learning and neural networks to help companies to bring treatments to market faster.

"Using AI to auto-generate a weekly status report or pick the top five emails in your inbox doesn't have the same wow factor as, say, curing a disease would, which is why these near-term, practical uses go unnoticed," said Craig Roth, Research Vice President at Gartner. "Companies are just beginning to seize the opportunity to improve non-routine work through AI by applying it to general-purpose tools. Once knowledge workers incorporate AI into their work processes as a virtual secretary or intern, robo-employees will become a competitive necessity."[36]

Leveraging technologies such as AI and robotics, retailers will use intelligent process automation to identify, optimize and automate labor-intensive and repetitive activities that

---

36   *ibid*

are currently performed by humans, reducing labor costs through efficiency from headquarters to distribution centers and stores. Many retailers are already expanding technology use to improve the in-store check-out process.

Through 2022, multichannel retailer efforts to replace sales associates through AI will prove unsuccessful, although cashier and operational jobs will be disrupted.

To take full advantage of this collaboration, companies must understand how humans can most effectively augment machines, how machines can enhance what humans do best, and how to redesign business processes to support the partnership.

At the World Economic Forum in Davos, Paul Daugherty, Accenture's Chief Technology and Innovation Officer summed this idea up as, "Human plus machine equals superpowers." Automation and artificial intelligence are transforming businesses and will contribute to economic growth via contributions to productivity.

MACHINES ASSISTING HUMANS

Smart machines are helping humans expand their abilities in three ways. They can *amplify* our cognitive strengths;

interact with customers and employees to free us for higher-level tasks; and *embody* human skills to extend our physical capabilities.

Amplifying—Artificial intelligence can boost our analytic and decision-making abilities by providing the right information at the right time. But it can also heighten creativity. Consider how Autodesk's Dreamcatcher AI enhances the imagination of even exceptional designers. A designer provides Dreamcatcher with criteria about the desired product—for example, a chair able to support up to 300 pounds, with a seat eighteen inches off the ground, made of materials costing less than $75, and so on.

Interacting—Human-machine collaboration enables companies to interact with employees and customers in novel, more effective ways. AI agents like Cortana, for example, can facilitate communications between people or on behalf of people, such as by transcribing a meeting and distributing a voice-searchable version to those who couldn't attend. Such applications are inherently scalable—a single chatbot, for instance, can provide routine customer service to large numbers of people simultaneously, wherever they may be.

Embodying—Many AIs, like Aida and Cortana, exist principally as digital entities, but in other applications the intelligence is embodied in a robot that augments a human worker.

With their sophisticated sensors, motors, and actuators, AI-enabled machines can now recognize people and objects and work safely alongside humans in factories, warehouses, and laboratories.[37]

THE RISE OF SUPERJOBS

As machines take over routine, repeatable tasks and people focus on more sophisticated work, traditional roles are evolving into hybrid jobs and "superjobs" performed with a powerful combination of human intelligence, AI, cognitive technology, and robotics.

The Deloitte 2019 Global Human Capital Trends survey bears this out. "Most respondents are using automation to eliminate transactional work and replace repetitive tasks, while nearly half are also augmenting existing work practices to improve productivity, and more than one-third are "reimagining work." Many are also doubling down on reskilling, investing in retraining to make automation truly effective and worthwhile."[38]

Forward-thinking companies are responding by redesigning jobs—along with business and work processes—to keep pace. In traditional job design, organizations create fixed, stable

---

37 *"How Humans And AI Are Working Together In 1,500 Companies".*
    2019. Harvard Business Review.
38 *"The Deloitte 2019 Global Human Capital Trends - 2019.*

roles with written job descriptions and then add management. When parts of a job are automated by machines, people perform the more interpretive and service-oriented work that remains. In contrast to fixed tasks, this work requires more flexible and less rigidly defined positions.

In today's job market, demand and wage acceleration are strongest for hybrid jobs requiring a blend of technical and soft skills, for example, technology operations and data analysis and interpretation combined with communication, service, and collaboration. These new job types—manager, designer, architect, analyst—are evolving into superjobs that leverage the significant productivity and efficiency gains possible when people work with smart machines, data, and algorithms. In a superjob, technology not only changes the skills the job requires; it changes the nature of the work itself.

FROM REDESIGNING JOBS TO RETHINKING WORK

Creating superjobs—deconstructing, recombining, and expanding existing roles—requires deeply rethinking work design. Simply automating existing tasks can increase throughput, but the potential is so much bigger: Redesigning jobs and work for a true marriage of human strengths and machine power can significantly improve customer service, output, and productivity.

- In the future, work will be defined by:

- Output and problems solved, not activities and tasks executed

- Teams and relationships engaged and motivated, not subordinates supervised

- Tools and technologies that both automate work and augment the workforce to increase productivity and enhance value to customers

- Integration of development, learning, and new experiences into the day-to-day (often real-time) flow of work

THE FUTURE OF COLLABORATION

Augmenting the workforce with robotics and AI technology will, no doubt, lead to new ways to get the job done. The challenge before organizations is to achieve this reinvention with positive results for businesses, working people, and the economy and society as a whole.

Let's examine some examples of organizations that are already making steps towards making their workforce more Symbiotic (Humans + Machines).

THE USS GABRIELLE GIFFORDS

The USS Gabrielle Giffords, rides high in the water on three separate hulls and is powered like a jet ski—that is, by water-breathing jets instead of propellers. This lets it move swiftly in the coastal shallows where it's meant to dominate.

Unlike the older Navy ships—the littoral combat ship was built on the concept of "modularity." There's a voluminous hollow in the ship's belly, and its insides can be swapped out in port, allowing it to set sail as a submarine hunter, mine-sweeper, or surface combatant, depending on the mission.

The ship's most futuristic aspect, though, is its crew. The LCS was the first class of Navy ship that, because of technological change and the high cost of personnel, turned away from specialists in favor of "hybrid sailors" who have the ability to acquire skills rapidly.[39]

It was designed to operate with a mere forty souls on board—one-fifth of the number aboard comparably sized "legacy" ships and far from the 350 aboard a World War II destroyer. The small size of the crew means that each sailor must be like the ship itself: a jack of many trades and not, as 240 years of tradition have prescribed, a master of just one.

---

39   *Useem, Jerry. 2019. "At Work, Expertise Is Falling Out Of Favor".*

Ten years from now, the Deloitte consultant Erica Volini projects, "70 to 90 percent of workers will be in so-called hybrid jobs or superjobs—that is, positions combining tasks once performed by people in two or more traditional roles. "[40]

SIEMENS:

"Millions of years ago, in prehistoric Africa, an early human picked up a stone and used it as a hammer. And so, the first tool was born. Today, in China, Zi Jian and his team have taken the next evolutionary step: through simple hand gestures they've taught robots to use tools for us."[41]

Imagine a world where robots and humans work side by side. Where you can command a robot to lift a box or pass a tool with absolute precision, using a simple hand gesture. Where the learning ability of humans and the accuracy and strength of robots work in harmony to make our lives easier, safer, and richer.

That's the vision of Zi Jian and his colleagues, a pioneering team researching and testing technologies for the future of manufacturing, as part of the Siemens "Autonomous Systems

---

40 *ibid*
41 *Services, Products, Market-specific Solutions, Topic Areas, Jobs Careers, Siemens Iraq, Siemens Lebanon, and Life Siemens et al. 2019. "Working With Robots: The Future Of Collaboration". Siemens Middle East.*

Revolution" Project. Hard at work at a lab in bustling Beijing, this world-class team is building a tool that lets humans and robots communicate. It has no keyboard and there isn't a touchscreen in sight. But with leading-edge thinking and smart technology they've opened up a channel of communication between man and machine.

For just over a year, Zi Jian has been working on the data glove, a tool that allows a person to control and command a robotic arm. Using different sensors, the glove captures and translates the movements and gestures of human hands—and, someday soon, their exact pressure levels—into actions that are performed by the hand of a robot. Through this clever mechanism a human can command a robot to pick up heavy objects, hand over tools and components, or assist in assembling parts of a product.

Pressure sensors on the tip of the robot's hand send feedback to the person wearing the glove, so touching an object through a robot's hand will feel the same as if you were touching it yourself. So, the intelligence and decision-making powers of humans are matched by the strength and precision of robots, allowing for ever more complex, delicate, and exciting possibilities.

Using gesture-based interactions, a car manufacturing worker will be able to direct a machine to assemble a car, sensing and feeling each part as if it were in their hands. Cumbersome, strenuous work will be carried out with grace, ease, and efficiency by our robot co-workers.[42]

"Once this channel of communication has been opened, it can be used to control anything you want." From robots that are trained to assist neurosurgeons during complicated brain surgery, to factory robots that take on the lifting and mixing of chemicals in a factory—vital tasks that can be hazardous to humans. The opportunities for human-robot collaboration are endless.

GOOGLE:

The recent victory of DeepMind's artificial intelligence over professional gamers in StarCraft II, may prompt many to wonder why Google's parent company, Alphabet, is investing hundreds of millions of dollars a year to play games. The simple answer is: intuition.

In this case, intuition means that the computer is able to act unconsciously, irrationally, and quickly, surpassing ordinary processing to deeply understand the information and the situation at hand. Given that these games have a nearly infinite

---

42 *ibid*

number of moves, DeepMind's successes show that the AI is aware of its environment and of other players.

This intuition is valuable beyond the gaming environment and is expected to be replicable in many aspects of society. It will be something that people will eventually interact with on a daily basis in their jobs. Just as one can play alongside the computer in a game, the same will be possible in the workplace.

In developing this technology, the AI improves through imitation learning, which imitates past trajectories, and self-play, observing the play of people and then playing against different versions of itself, each time learning from the best player in previous iterations. It's much the same way that humans learn, except that the AI learns much faster.

In observing how players win at games, the AI learns from their successes and failures. Similarly, AI will be used to identify how employees succeed and make mistakes in their jobs. The AI will then be able to help employees in preventing mistakes before they happen. This could be as simple as making sure that all aspects of a form are filled out correctly, or as complex as creating the foundation for an investment bank's financial model.

This technology won't remove the human component entirely, but it does have the potential to automate a significant portion of the work involved. In observing how the best employees do their job, AI will be able to create a framework for how that job should be performed. Just as AI in a video game can observe winning players' behavior and then use the most effective strategies and tactics to win the game.

The difference, of course, is that real life isn't a game. People will still play an important part in all functions within a business. The real-world changes constantly, and that requires someone to make sure that any AI-created framework is suitable for particular circumstances.

AMAZON

Another example of a company where human workers and robots work side by side is Amazon. "Orange robots, about the size of a big suitcase, buzz through the Amazon sortation center in Denver, Colorado. Conveyor belts on top of the robots look like a mini treadmill for packages that are delivered to one of hundreds of chutes in the warehouse. Amazon associates rely on software to guide the company's newest robotic drive units, which help get packages to customers more quickly."[43]

"If you had told 10-year-old me that my job would revolve around robots every day, there's no way I would have believed

---

43   "New Robots, New Jobs". 2019. US Day One Blog.

you," said Cathryn Kachura, an Amazon employee who keeps the robots running.

Kachura is one of five flow control specialists at Amazon's Denver sortation center, where customer packages from the company's fulfillment centers are sorted by zip code before they're sent out for delivery. Her job is to manage inbound and outbound package volume and distribution. But she doesn't do it alone. She and her team rely on roughly 800 robotic drive units to do a lot of the heavy lifting. "We employ the same number of people now that we did before we had the robotics field. The robots just pick up the extra workload."

Resembling an orange nightstand on wheels, the two-feet-high, 3-feet-wide Pegasus drive is Amazon's newest robot designed to create greater efficiency in its sortation process so customers can receive their orders even faster. They represent Amazon's highest ever drive density in its network, requiring the need for "robot traffic control."

Steve Campbell, director of Amazon Robotics Product Strategy, was leading the team as these robotics were developed and deployed. "After months of hard work and testing, it is exciting to see this robotic solution come to life and to meet the flow controllers like Cathryn who monitor the health of the system. The robotic system will increase the building capacity, and as it scales we will need to hire more people to help sustain the increased productivity levels. This is the chain reaction of job growth we strive for when designing robotic systems."

HAVING A ROBOT AS A COLLEAGUE

As we see more and more companies integrating AI and automation in their daily operation, we realize that working with robots is not a future fantasy any more, it's happening right now, and it's expected to increase in the next few years. But while robots can make us more productive and easier to do our job, how do you feel about having a robot as a colleague?

A few years ago, researchers explored how people feel about having robots for colleagues, the researchers set out to examine whether cultural differences may exist in the acceptance of robotic colleagues between German and American workers. They didn't find much in the way of national differences, but they did reveal some interesting thoughts on life with a robotic colleague.

For instance, "over 60 percent of respondents could easily imagine being supported by a robotic colleague, with 21 percent even suggesting such a change would be an improvement, with this largely due to the belief that a robot would be less error prone and more predictable in their behavior."[44]

---

44 *Kshirsagar, Alap, Bnaya Dreyfuss, Guy Ishai, Ori Heffetz, and Guy Hoffman. 2019. "Monetary-Incentive Competition Between Humans And Robots: Experimental Results".*

A recent study from Cornell University suggests this is not quite so clear cut, however. It explored how people feel when they're working alongside robots, and the robot turns out to be better at their job than them. It emerged that being beaten by a machine tends to make people feel badly about themselves and their abilities, which in turn makes them resent the machines.

"Think about a cashier working side-by-side with an automatic check-out machine, or someone operating a forklift in a warehouse which also employs delivery robots driving right next to them," the researchers say. "While it may be tempting to design such robots for optimal productivity, engineers and managers need to take into consideration how the robots' performance may affect the human workers' effort and attitudes toward the robot and even toward themselves. Our research is the first that specifically sheds light on these effects."

Research from the University of Lincoln found that when robots were made with similar human flaws and foibles, volunteers were better able to bond with and form an emotional attachment to them. Does this mean that humans cannot form any kind of emotional attachment to robots? Perhaps not, with research published in nature highlighting the compassion and empathy people can feel for robots.

After wiring volunteers up to an EEG to monitor their brain activity, they were able to show that people exposed to images of a robotic hand in a painful situation exhibited empathy towards the robot. Granted, the empathy wasn't on the same level as they showed to humans, but it was there nonetheless.

A MACHINE MAY NOT TAKE YOUR JOB, BUT ONE COULD BECOME YOUR BOSS

When Conor Sprouls, a customer service representative in the call center of the insurance giant MetLife talks to a customer over the phone, he keeps one eye on the bottom-right corner of his screen. There, in a little blue box, A.I. tells him how he's doing. Talking too fast? The program flashes an icon of a speedometer, indicating that he should slow down. Sound sleepy? The software displays an "energy cue," with a picture of a coffee cup. Not empathetic enough? A heart icon pops up.

For years people have imagined hyper-efficient robots invading offices and factories and working as our colleague. However, we may have overlooked the possibility it will replace the bosses, too.

Mr. Sprouls and the other call center workers at his office in Warwick, R.I., still have plenty of human supervisors. But the software on their screens—made by Cogito, an AI company in Boston—has become a kind of adjunct manager, always watching them. At the end of every call, Mr. Sprouls's Cogito notifications are tallied and added to a statistics dashboard that his supervisor can view. If he hides the Cogito window by minimizing it, the program notifies his supervisor.[45]

The goal of automation has always been efficiency, but in this new kind of workplace, AI sees humanity itself as the thing to be optimized.

Cogito, which works with large insurance companies such as MetLife and Humana as well as financial and retail firms, says it has 20,000 users. Percolata, a Silicon Valley company that counts Uniqlo and 7-Eleven among its clients, uses in-store sensors to calculate a "true productivity" score for each worker, and ranks workers from most to least productive.

Management by algorithm is not a new concept. In the early twentieth century, Frederick Winslow Taylor revolutionized the manufacturing world with his "scientific management" theory, which tried to wring inefficiency out of factories by timing and measuring each aspect of a job. More recently, Uber, Lyft and other on-demand platforms have made billions of dollars by outsourcing conventional tasks of human resources—scheduling, payroll, performance reviews— to computers.

---

45 *"A Machine May Not Take Your Job, But One Could Become Your Boss". 2019. Nytimes.Com.*

But using AI to manage workers in conventional, nine to five jobs has been more controversial. Critics have accused companies of using algorithms for managerial tasks, saying that automated systems can dehumanize and unfairly punish employees. While it's clear why executives would want AI that can track everything their workers do, it's less clear why workers would.

Defenders of workplace AI might argue that these systems are not meant to be overbearing. Instead, they're meant to make workers better by reminding them to thank the customer, to empathize with the frustrated claimant on Line 1 or to avoid slacking off on the job.

The best argument for workplace AI may be situations in which human bias skews decision making, such as hiring. Pymetrics, a New York start-up, has made inroads in the corporate hiring world by replacing the traditional résumé screening process with an AI program that uses a series of games to test for relevant skills. The algorithms are then analyzed to make sure they are not creating biased hiring outcomes or favoring one group over another.

* * *

At the moment, we are still at an early stage in our understanding of how man and machine function alongside one another, and so findings such as these remain novel and exciting. As man and machine begin to work increasingly in unison, it's vital that we gain a greater understanding of the nature of the interactions between them.

Considerable time and energy have been devoted to ensuring that human employees work effectively together, but perhaps now the time has come for similar energy to be devoted to ensuring man and machine can do likewise.

CHAPTER 3

NEW SKILLS FOR NEW ECONOMIES

————

- Artificial Intelligence Skills Shortage

- Tech Companies Are Partnering with Higher Educational Institutions to Close the Education Gap

- Tech Skills Are in Demand, But Companies Can't Lose Sight of Soft Skills

ARTIFICIAL INTELLIGENCE SKILLS SHORTAGE

Now that nearly every company is considering how AI applications can positively impact their businesses, they are on the hunt for professionals to help them make their vision a reality.

The expanding applications for AI have created a shortage of qualified workers in the field. Although schools across the country are adding classes, increasing enrollment, and developing new programs to accommodate student demand, there are too few potential employees with training or experience in AI.

As the democratization of artificial intelligence applications expands as a possibility not just for tech giants, but now viable for small- and medium-sized businesses, the demand for AI professionals to do the work has ballooned as well. The corporate management's excitement for AI's various applications is building and then once they have bought into the concept (which is happening much more rapidly), they want to make it real right away.

According to the World Economic Forum's Future of Jobs Report 2018, "8 million net new jobs will be created because of the emergence of AI"[46]. But there's obviously a disconnect between how AI and machine learning jobs are trending and the actual skills availability—or even interest—in the labor force.

That has big consequences. Too few AI-trained job seekers have slowed hiring and impeded growth at some companies.

---

46 *"Machines Will Do More Tasks Than Humans By 2025 But Robot Revolution Will Still Create 58 Million Net New Jobs In Next Five Years". 2019. World Economic Forum.s*

It may also be delaying broader adoption of a technology that some economists say could spur U.S. economic growth by boosting productivity, currently growing at only about half its precise pace.

Chinese tech giant Tencent, in a study compiled by its research institute, estimates there are around "300,000 AI professionals in the world—but millions more are needed." [47]While these are speculative figures, the competitive salaries and benefits packages and the aggressive recruiting tactics rolled out by firms to recruit AI talent would suggest the supply of AI talent is nowhere near matching up to the demand. In fact, Silicon Valley giants are fighting and paying an exorbitant amount of money to lure the best AI engineers to work for them.

"Typical A.I. specialists, including both Ph.D.s fresh out of school and people with less education and just a few years of experience, can be paid from $300,000 to $500,000 a year or more in salary and company stock".[48] Well-known names in the A.I. field have received compensation in salary and shares in a company's stock that total single- or double-digit millions over a four- or five-year period. And at some point, they renew or negotiate a new contract, much like a professional athlete.

---

47   *"Tencent Says There Are Only 300,000 AI Engineers Worldwide, But Millions Are Needed". 2019. The Verge.*

48   *"Tech Giants Are Paying Huge Salaries For Scarce A.I. Talent". 2019. Nytimes.Com.*

Salaries are spiraling so fast that some joke the tech industry needs a National Football League-style salary cap on A.I. specialists. "That would make things easier," said Christopher Fernandez, one of Microsoft's hiring managers. "A lot easier."

Figure-7: AI experts

Wanted: Artificial intelligence experts

In artificial intelligence, job openings are rising faster than job seekers.

There is a shortage of talent, and the big companies are trying to land as much of it as they can. Solving tough A.I. problems is not like building the flavor-of-the-month smartphone app. In the entire world, fewer than 10,000 people have the skills necessary to tackle serious artificial intelligence research, according to Element AI, an independent lab in Montreal.

To move AI projects from ideation into implementation, companies will need to determine how to close the AI skills gap, so they have experts on their team to get the job done.

HOW TO CLOSE THE GAP?

Instead of upping the salaries to millions of dollars and fighting for the same small pool of talent, we should be training engineers in artificial intelligence around the world. Young students and engineers in remote developing countries also have the ability to perform—and, at times, outperform—the ones who have degrees from elite institutions in the West. There is untapped talent in these places, and we are neglecting it to our detriment.

"Educating engineers from across the globe in machine learning, deep learning, and natural language processing—the most common sub-disciplines within AI—will help increase access to AI talent. Someone who experiences complex problems in his or her own country could be more suited to try and solve those problems with AI. For example, a Nepali engineer who wants to use machine learning to predict crop yields of their community will be better informed about Nepal's farmlands than a graduate from Silicon Valley."[49]

But how do we train local engineers in far-flung places to build drones, robots, and complex systems?

The answer is in a combination of online courses and some onsite training.

---

49 *"Council Post: Here's Why We Need To Democratize Artificial Intelligence". 2019. Forbes.Com.*

Two years ago, Fuse machines launched a fellowship program that allows students in Nepal to develop high-level skills in programming and solving machine learning algorithms—eventually leading to a Micro Masters in Artificial Intelligence from Columbia University. Today, the program has expanded to three additional locations: the Dominican Republic, New York City, and Rwanda.

As they complete the course, enrolled students come to class once a week and discuss the homework assignments and problems. What they've found is that this mix of an online course with onsite guidance works very well with the students. They learn on their own time throughout the week, but still feel like a part of a class when they meet with other students in a physical location. With this model of learning, many engineers graduate with certificates in AI from Columbia University.[50]

Thanks to the emerging edtech revolution, a student from a poor village in Rwanda now has the same opportunities as a third-generation legacy Yale student. The playing field has been levelled in a way that's truly unprecedented in history. The best educators in the world are now available to everyone. Online platforms such as MIT OpenCourseWare, Coursera, and even YouTube grant access to some of the best instructors in the globe. A student living in an isolated rural area,

---

50 *ibid*

or even in the far reaches of Africa, can now attend lectures by prestigious professors at Harvard, Yale, or MIT.

As the technologies of the Fourth Industrial Revolution create new pressures on labor markets, education reform, lifelong learning, and reskilling initiatives will be key to ensuring both that individuals have access to economic opportunity by remaining competitive in the new world of work, and that businesses have access to the talent they need for the jobs of the future.

According to World Economic Forum founder and executive chairman Klaus Schwab: "It is critical that business take an active role in supporting their existing workforces through reskilling and upskilling, that individuals take a proactive approach to their own lifelong learning, and that governments create an enabling environment to facilitate this workforce transformation. This is the key challenge of our time."[51]

TECH COMPANIES ARE PARTNERING WITH HIGHER EDUCATIONAL INSTITUTIONS TO CLOSE THE SKILL GAP

Despite rapidly expanding access to educational resources, academic training alone is insufficient to bridge the skills

---

51 *"Machines Will Do More Tasks Than Humans By 2025 But Robot Revolution Will Still Create 58 Million Net New Jobs In Next Five Years"*. 2019. World Economic Forum.

gap. Academic training must be paired with occupational experience to create seasoned, talented professionals who are able to operate in leadership roles.

Upgrading skills should match the pace of technological change and retraining should be accessed when needed. "As much as 82 percent of executives at companies with more than USD 100 million in annual revenues believe retraining and reskilling to be at least half of the answer to addressing their skills gap."[52]

While the academic world isn't moving fast enough to fulfil market needs, and close the skills gap, tech companies are stepping up to create partnerships with universities to help bridge the education gap.

MICROSOFT UPSKILLING INITIATIVES

Microsoft and General Assembly are looking to lessen the skills gap with a new initiative. The two companies have announced a new partnership for skills in AI, machine learning, cloud and data engineering, data science, among others.

"The initiative will aim to build credentials and standards for AI skills, upskill and reskill 15,000 workers by 2022, along

---

52 *"Retraining And Reskilling Workers In The Age Of Automation".*
    2019. Mckinsey & Company.

with creating a pool of AI talent for the global workforce. According to both firms, the joint program will be focused on three main areas: setting the standards for AI skills, developing scalable AI training solutions for firms, and building a sustainable talent pool of workers with AI skills."[53]

Karen Kocher, General Manager of 21st Century Jobs, Skills and Employability at Microsoft, noted the importance of these collaborations in the following manner:

"The incredible transformation we're witnessing in the 21st century workplace calls out the need for organizations—governments, higher education institutions, employers, the nonprofit sector—to step up and tackle one of the fundamental challenges of our time: closing the skills gap by teaching, training and preparing workers for the jobs of tomorrow."

Here are few examples of institutions collaborating with Microsoft:

- Bellevue College is offering a blended and flex-learning model in AI, big data, data science, and cybersecurity based on Microsoft courses

---

53 Center, Microsoft. 2019. "Microsoft And General Assembly Launch Partnership To Close The Global AI Skills Gap - Stories".

- Purdue University Global will grant credits toward a full degree when students complete Microsoft technical skills programs in areas like AI, cybersecurity, data science, and more

- London School of Economics and Political Science is embedding data science skills and knowledge into first-year students' curriculum

- Staffordshire University is delivering Microsoft courses across their student population, integrating modules as part of their "Staffordshire Award" employability program

- University of London is integrating the Microsoft Professional Program in Data Science into its new MSc Data Science degree course

These higher educational institutions will essentially be integrating the technical programs into their curricula, including courses on AI, Data Science, Cyber Security, and Computer Science. Not only will cost-effective educational choices be provided to students, but their skill set will be polished with the specific aim of helping them become well-trained professionals in technical fields that the job market increasingly requires in this day and age.

Partnership will upskill and reskill 15,000 workers over the next three years and create industry-recognized credentials for AI skills.

"To ensure that businesses can meet ever-growing AI talent needs, GA and Microsoft will establish an AI Talent Network to source candidates for hire and project-based work. GA will leverage its existing network of twenty-two campuses and the broader Adecco ecosystem to create a repeatable talent pipeline for the AI Talent Network."

AMAZON WEB SERVICES PARTNERS WITH GEORGE MASON

Amazon Web Services partners with George Mason on four-year cloud degree program.

The company has entered a partnership with George Mason University to create a four-year bachelor's degree program focused on cloud computing." Says AWS worldwide public sector business chief, Teresa Carlson

"Developing a cloud-ready workforce is an urgent challenge and an incredible opportunity. The bachelor's degree offering from George Mason University is a powerful extension of the work at Northern Virginia Community College, and a seminal contribution to AWS Educate's global cloud degree offering," Carlson said in a statement.[54]

GMU's BAS degree will focus on technical skills such as cloud architecture, cybersecurity, software development, and DevOps through a curriculum developed in collaboration with AWS Educate, the cloud vendor's higher education initiative that provides resources to colleges and universities.

"It is essential that in this revolution in computing that we call cloud computing that we figure out ways for everybody, regardless of their background, to find a way into the opportunities in this field," GMU President Ángel Cabrera said onstage. "The industry needs it, our economy needs it and, of course, it's the right thing to do to make sure there are no barriers to anyone."

In a release detailing the degree program, executives said it would be "backwards-mapped" to meet the in-demand skills, providing students with AWS Competency-based credentials and experience with new cloud technologies through membership in its AWS Educate program.

---

54 *2019. Bizjournals.Com. https://www.bizjournals.com/washington/ news/2019/06/11/amazon-web-services-partners-with-george- mason-on.html.*

THE UNIVERSITY OF LOUISVILLE AND IBM

The University of Louisville and IBM signed an agreement to establish the IBM Skills Academy, scheduled to open this fall at UL's Center for Digital Transformation. The partnership is one more example of the accelerating trend of universities and corporations teaming up to provide skills training for undergraduates considering possible employment in the technology sector.

"The academy will focus on emerging digital fields like artificial intelligence, cybersecurity, data science, blockchain, cloud technology, the Internet of Things, and quantum computing. Through the partnership, valued at $5 million annually, UL faculty and students will have access to a front-edge curriculum, software, industry experts, and other educational materials. IBM will train selected UL faculty in the content. The faculty, in turn, will instruct students who can earn IBM certificates and college credits."

"The UL/IBM partnership is a first of its kind, but it won't be the last." According to the Louisville Courier Journal, Naguib Attia, IBM vice president for global programs, indicated that the company planned to open three more skills academies at U.S. universities, modeled on the UL prototype.

MUTUALLY BENEFICIAL PARTNERSHIPS

It's not hard to understand why this partnership was formed and why expansion will occur. Like-purposed skills academies serve at least four aims, each mutually beneficial to their university and corporate partners.

1. A Boost for Economic Development: The academy helps address the continuing digital divide between plentiful technology jobs and the lack of skilled workers who can succeed in them. This is particularly important in small towns and regions like Kentucky where jobs in traditional industries are being lost even as positions in the tech sector either go unfilled or are developing more slowly than in competitor locations.

2. A Recruiting Advantage for Universities: As the number of high school graduates decrease and the unemployment rate remains low, colleges are facing an increasingly competitive environment in which to maintain their enrollments. Supplementing traditional majors with boot camp style technology skills training offers a "two-for-one" marketing strategy for colleges attempting to recover or ramp up enrollment.

3. A Source of Talent for Companies: Companies invest millions of dollars searching for talented employees, and they commit millions more in training workers in

the critical skills necessary for job success and company progress. Skills academies like the UL/IBM initiative will give the employer partner a head start—and a smart start—on both tasks.

4. A Combined Purpose for Education: College students express two major motives for pursuing their education—to prepare themselves for a good job and to gain knowledge so they are broadly prepared for a successful life. Although job preparation is currently the predominant aim among collegians, institutions that find ways to provide students with both purposes will be the most likely to thrive.

TECH SKILLS ARE IN DEMAND, BUT COMPANIES CAN'T LOSE SIGHT OF SOFT SKILLS

There are no limits when people power technology—we break barriers and unleash true transformation. But we also need resourceful, gritty people who can grapple with problems that are more complex and nuanced than that can be solved with formulaic, push-button solutions. While digital competencies like coding are essential to the workforce of the future, we must balance them with those who can think holistically about problems, find innovative solutions that reflect experience, and that have a voice to articulate and gain consensus.

Putting digital tools into the hands of our people is essential. But even more impactful is having the right team leaders in place. They play a crucial role in the experience employees have at their company—and in cultivating and retaining top talent. Empathy is a critical trait in effective leaders as they help their people balance personal and professional fulfillment. The leaders who approach their team(s) with openness and compassion, and who demonstrate the capacity to understand and communicate around the biggest challenges and opportunities facing their people, are more likely to lead engaged, effective teams. Employees who buy in thanks to effective leaders are often those who cultivate the relationships that create synergies between teams, contribute to team culture and morale. They feel safe thinking outside the box to come up with new ways to make an impact with their clients and beyond.

THE MOST INVALUABLE SKILLS IN THE AGE OF ROBOTS

According to Martin Ford, the author of *Architects of Intelligence,* the best way to prepare for the job automation is to transition away from things that are largely routine and predictable and try to find a role that is largely focused on tasks that are not easy to automate.

Martin also suggests three areas:

1. *Creative work*—where you are building something new, thinking outside the box in nonpredictable ways, etc.

2. *Human-centered work*—where you build sophisticated relationships with people. This would include caring roles, as with a nurse or social worker, but also business roles where you need to have an understanding of your clients.

3. *Skilled trade work*—this includes jobs that require lots of mobility, dexterity, and flexibility in unpredictable environments. Examples would be electricians or plumbers. Building a robot that can do these jobs is probably far in the future.

Another important part, according to Ford, is to realize that future careers will nearly all require continuous learning. So, a focus on learning, getting good at it, and truly enjoying it, will be one of the most important components of success.[55]

Take for example the automotive giant Toyota which is removing robots from its factories because human workers can, unlike their machine counterparts, propose ideas for improvement.

---

55 *"How Can We Best Prepare For Job Automation?". 2019. Medium.*

Machines, it seems, are not very good with innovation. They're not very good at certain types of agility, either. Watch Parisian waiters in action and ask yourself how long it would take for robots to put them out of a job. Then there's empathy, creativity, leadership, intuition, and social intelligence.

David Deming, associate professor of education and economics at Harvard University, argues that soft skills such as sharing, and negotiating will be crucial. He says the modern workplace, where people move between different roles and projects, closely resembles preschool classrooms, where we learn social skills such as empathy and cooperation.

Deming has mapped the changing needs of employers and identified key skills that will be required to thrive in the job market of the near future. Along with those soft skills, mathematical ability will be enormously beneficial.[56]

56 *"The Jobs Of The Future – And Two Skills You Need To Get Them".*
    2019. World Economic Forum.

Figure-8: Skills

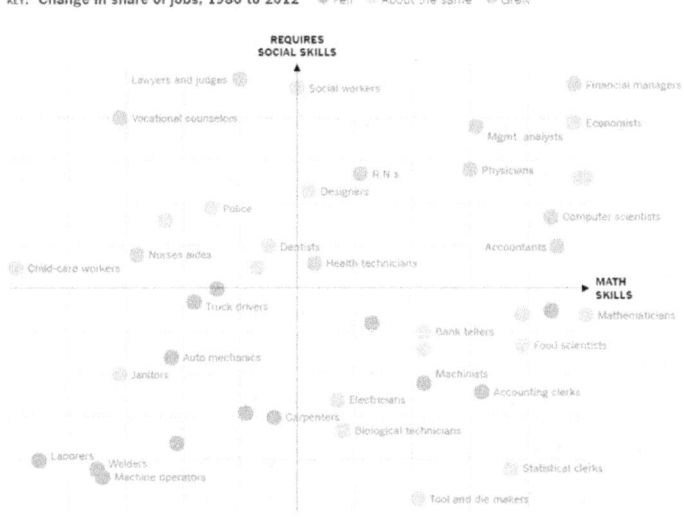

Source: David Deming, Harvard University

Deming shows that in recent years, many jobs requiring only mathematical skills have been automated. Bank tellers and statistical clerks have suffered. Roles which require predominantly social skills (childcare workers, for example) tend to be poorly paid as the supply of potential workers is very large.

The study shows that workers who successfully combine mathematical and interpersonal skills in the knowledge-based economies of the future should find many rewarding and lucrative opportunities. The challenge now, says Deming, is for educators to complement their teaching of technical skills like mathematics and computer science, with a focus on making sure the workers of the future have the soft skills to compete in the new jobs market.

THE TOP EMERGING SKILLS FOR THE FUTURE OF WORK

The World Economic Forum predicts that by 2022, 42 percent of required workplace skills will have changed. The emerging jobs for 2022 include roles based on technological innovation, like software and applications developers, and roles requiring distinctly "human" traits, like sales professionals. Not surprisingly, these jobs will require both various forms of technological competency, like programming and systems analysis, and distinctly "human" skills, like emotional intelligence, creativity, and critical thinking.

ACCORDING TO THE REPORT, HERE ARE THE TOP TEN EMERGING SKILLS FOR 2022:

1. Analytical thinking and innovation

2. Active learning and learning strategies

3. Creativity, originality, and initiative

4. Technology design and programming

5. Critical thinking and analysis

6. Complex problem solving

7. Leadership and social influence

8. Emotional intelligence

9. Reasoning, problem solving

10. Systems analysis and evaluation

The report suggests that before 2022, employees will need roughly 101 days of retraining and upskilling. And because the half-life of a professional skill is just five years, employees will need to become lifelong learners to remain competitive in the workplace.

The need for certain skill sets will rise. The difference between the abilities (demand) that employers want, and those that are currently available in the market (supply) will increase (skill gap) and create a huge problem for both employers and potential employees.

So, what skills are candidates lacking? You'd think employers struggle to find applicants with hard skills like financial modeling, six-sigma, or programming, but after LinkedIn surveyed 5,000 talent professionals in thirty-five different countries, the largest gap was actually in soft skills. That term is thrown around quite a bit. In a nutshell, soft skills are one's ability to interact with other people effectively. Doesn't seem hard, but in reality, many candidates spend a great deal of time preparing for the technical components of the job and forget the importance of these qualitative abilities.[57]

HERE ARE THE TOP FIVE SOFT SKILLS
ACCORDING TO LINKEDIN:

1. *Creativity:* Creativity, as defined by LinkedIn, is the ability to solve problems in original ways. A skill that was historically associated with designers, artists, and marketing professionals is now an ability that's a requirement of every role. As the world becomes more automated and managed by machines, the ability to think outside the box will become a competitive advantage.

2. *Persuasion:* Persuasion is one's ability to sway others to their point of view. Regardless of your profession or role, your success often depends on how well you can motivate, inspire, and engage others in your ideas. Especially in leadership positions, it's critical that managers create buy-in and can advance the ideas of their teams.

---

57 *"Linkedin Surveyed 5,000 Talent Professionals And Found The Top 3 Ways Employers Are Screening For Soft Skills". 2019. Inc.Com.*

3. *Collaboration:* Collaborative work environments are quickly becoming the new norm. Companies are redesigning their offices, rewriting their policies, and investing in technologies to facilitate teamwork. Not only does collaboration create a more enjoyable work environment, but it also results in tangible business advantages.

4. *Adaptability:* You've heard it before—the only thing that's consistent is change. Unless you possess the ability to adapt, adjust, and embrace change, you'll be left in the dust as your industry and company evolves.

5. *Time Management:* We all have to juggle multiple tasks at work. If you're not careful, competing priorities, individual agendas, and interruptions can negatively affect your ability to make progress in the areas important to the business. In a world where time is now the most valuable resource, one's capability to effectively manage their day is an advantage.

* * *

Soft skills are now more important than ever. So much so that 80 percent of those surveyed by LinkedIn say they are growing in importance to business success, while 89 percent highlighted a lack of soft skills among bad hires at their organization.

The challenge for employers, however, is that soft skills can be hard to identify in the recruitment process. It's often only when someone is in-post that soft skills become evident or their absence is revealed. The unstructured, pre-hire assessment of soft skills is a significant problem, with 68 percent telling LinkedIn the main way they assess them is by picking up on social cues in interviews.

That's an approach that relies on the interviewee presenting an authentic version of themselves, unaffected by interview nerves or excitement, and on the interviewer being a reliable interpreter of social cues. Employers need to start formalizing their approach to soft skills assessments, by having a clear idea of what skills they need, then using AI tools to analyze the extent to which candidates have those skills.

CHAPTER 4

THE DISRUPTION IN HIGHER EDUCATION

- Why Is Higher Education Ripe for Disruption?

- The Student Debt Crisis

- Higher Education Return on Investment

- Will College and Graduate Programs Still Be Relevant in the Future?

- The Class of 2030

WHY IS HIGHER EDUCATION
RIPE FOR DISRUPTION?

THE HISTORY OF THE ACADEMIC DEGREE

The familiar formal degree titles such as bachelor's, master's, and doctorates were developed in Europe during the High Middle Ages. Oxford University was constructed in the eleventh century, with Cambridge following in the thirteenth. The tradition of an institution awarding formal degree titles continues today. The most exclusive schools offer the most exclusive degrees which carry the most prestige. Being admitted to an exclusive school is about gaining access to the knowledge and wisdom that they contain. One tries to gain access to the best possible resources for the hope of a better future.

However, we could argue that the greatest repository of human knowledge is now no longer a particular school, library, or degree program. It is the Internet. Armed with a computer and an Internet connection, a self-motivated individual could, in theory, teach themselves anything that they want to know. At the time of this writing, the English version of Wikipedia alone has over 5 million articles. Compare that to the library of just 320 volumes that were bequeathed by John Harvard for the founding of the eponymous university in 1636.

However, with no formal syllabus or curriculum, the self-learner would find themselves overwhelmed by the amount of information online. Where would they start? What is essential information and what is merely supplementary? What is a trusted source, and what is incorrect? Autodidactism, the act of self-education without teachers or institutions, is a rare skill possessed by the most self-motivated and often the most naturally gifted. We could not expect everyone on the planet to learn unaided.

The process of finding the most valuable information and ensuring a steady progression through concepts of increasing complexity, is a key that traditional education institutions still hold: decades of teaching and proven feedback loops, informed by the latest research, keeps syllabuses up to date. Teachers can also observe and interact with learners to gauge their understanding of the material and help them progress if they are stuck.

Clearly, our schools and colleges offer a learning experience far greater than self-learning via the Internet, regardless of the ease of access to the material. They also reward those that graduate with formal qualifications or accreditations which have become the societal norm for acceptance into graduate schemes and prestigious jobs.

However, is it possible to imagine a future where the Internet could be used as a delivery mechanism of world-class education, regardless of the student's location or background? Can we lower the barrier of entry to education through technology and educate the world in a democratized manner?

WHO EVEN NEEDS A DEGREE?

Given that most students attend university to maximize their chances of landing a good career, could it be possible that they could achieve this without going to a university at all? Whereas some fields still require lengthy formal education, such as medicine, other fields are beginning to relax the constraints on employment. Fueled by the high demand for talent, technology companies are beginning to look at other ways in which they can fill entry-level positions apart from targeting those that are graduating from computer science programs.

The future of education won't be about degrees. More and more, it'll be about skills. And no one school, whether it be Harvard, General Assembly, or Udacity, can ever insulate us from the unpredictability of technological progression and disruption. Google, for example, used to ask applicants for their college GPAs and transcripts; however, as Laszlo Bock—its head of hiring—has explained, those metrics aren't valuable predictors of an employee's performance. As a result, Bock told The New York Times a few years ago that the portion of noncollege-educated employees at Google has grown over time.[58]

Ernst & Young, has announced it will be removing the degree classification from its entry criteria, saying there is

---

58 "The Future Of Work Won't Be About College Degrees, It Will Be About Job Skills". 2019. CNBC.

"no evidence" success at university correlates with achievement in later life. Maggie Stilwell, EY's managing partner for talent, said the company would use online assessments to judge the potential of applicants. "Academic qualifications will still be taken into account and indeed remain an important consideration when assessing candidates as a whole but will no longer act as a barrier to getting a foot in the door," she said.[59]

Harvard Business School professor, Clayton Christensen, and co-author, Henry Eyring, analyzed the future of traditional universities in their book *The Innovative University*, and conclude that online education will become a more cost-effective way for students to receive an education, effectively undermining the business models of traditional institutions and running them out of business.[60]

At the Innovation + Disruption Symposium in Higher Education in 2017, Christensen specifically predicted that "50 percent of the 4,000 colleges and universities in the U.S. will either merge or close in the next 10 to 15 years." More recently, he doubled down on his statements, telling 1,500 attendees at Salesforce.org's Higher Education

59 Lucy Sherriff, ernst-and-young-removes-degree-classification-entry-criteria, Huffingtonpost.Co.Uk. 2019.

60 Christensen, Clayton M, and Henry J Eyring. The Innovative University : Changing the DNA of Higher Education from the inside Out. San Francisco, Jossey-Bass, 2011.=

Summit, "If you're asking whether the providers get disrupted within a decade - I might bet that it takes nine years rather than 10."[61]

* * *

The disruption is being driven by several converging forces: the unsustainable rise in college tuition, a change in consumer demand among prospective students, extreme negativity about the work readiness of college graduates, an unpacking of what makes college effective (work-integrated and relationship-rich), and emerging talent attraction and development strategies by employers. These signs and signals pointing toward a more direct employer-student model of higher education are already emerging.

THE STUDENT DEBT CRISIS

This topic is worth an entire book dedicated entirely to this subject, but I'll try to share some of the highlights that make the student debt one of the most important factors driving the education disruption.

---

61 Hess, Abigail. 2019. "Harvard Business School Professor: Half Of American Colleges Will Be Bankrupt In 10 To 15 Years". CNBC.

WHAT IS STUDENT DEBT?

Going to university in the United States is expensive—costing an average of over $34,000 a year in tuition and fees at private universities—which means for most Americans, the only way of viably pursuing higher education is to take out a student loan.

The figures are staggering. An estimated 45 million Americans have student loans, contributing to an overall national student debt of $1.6 trillion.[62]

WHAT STUDENT LOANS ARE AVAILABLE?

The two main options for prospective students are a government-funded federal loan or a private loan from a provider such as a bank, university, or state agency. Both are paid back with interest (interest on federal loans is fixed and normally lower than on private loans, which can be expensive and risky and comprise just 14 percent of student loans).

Federal loans come in various forms—including direct subsidized, direct unsubsidized, and direct plus for graduates and professionals. There's also Direct Plus for parents, where, as the name suggests, the student's guardians take the full burden.

---

62 *"Student Loan Debt Statistics In 2019: A $1.5 Trillion Crisis".
2019. Forbes.Com.*

Depending on year and dependency status, undergrads can borrow between $5,500 and $12,500 a year in federal loans; professionals and graduate students have access to up to $20,500 a year. Federal loan repayments are monthly and start six months after graduation—usually continuing for ten to twenty-five years.[63]

HOW MUCH IS THE AVERAGE STUDENT DEBT IN THE UNITED STATES?

The class of 2017 left college with an average of $28,650 each in debt, according to a report by the Institute for College Access and Success (TICAS). [64]This is a huge rise compared with the equivalent figure for just two decades ago. In 1996, the average debt of four-year students was less than half of that, at $12,750, the not-for-profit higher education organization found.

At an average of $37,000, student debt in America is high, but it is higher in the UK where the average is $55,000, according to analysis by YaleGlobal[65]. In stark contrast, students in Germany can expect to pay $2,200 for an undergraduate degree and come away with an average of $2,400 in debt.

---

63 *"Loans". 2019. Federal Student Aid.*
64 *"Student Debt And The Class Of 2017 - The Institute For College Access & Success". 2019. The Institute For College Access & Success.*
65 *"Student Debt Rising Worldwide | Yaleglobal Online". 2019. Yaleglobal.Yale.Edu.*

WHY IS THE U.S. STUDENT LOAN SYSTEM BROKEN?

As mentioned above, 45 million Americans have student loans and currently owe close to $1.6 trillion in student loans, an average of $34,000 per person. Over 2 million of them have defaulted on their loans in just the past six years, and the number grows by 1,400 a day. After years of projecting big profits from student lending, the federal government now acknowledges that taxpayers stand to lose $31.5 billion on the program over the next decade, and the losses are growing rapidly.[66]

Meanwhile, four in ten recent college graduates are in jobs that don't require a degree, according to the New York Federal Reserve. Many American colleges are dropout factories: At more than a third of them, less than half of the students who enroll earn a credential within eight years, according to the think tank Third Way.

The United States is shoveling more and more money into a highly inefficient system that, polls find, Americans are increasingly dissatisfied with. College tuition has soared 1,375 percent since 1978, more than four times the rate of overall inflation, Labor Department data show. Meanwhile, college presidents are being handsomely rewarded for the success of their enterprises: Seventy of them, including a dozen at public colleges, earned over $1 million in 2016–17, according to the Chronicle of Higher Education.

---

66 Mitchell, Josh. 2019. "The Long Road To The Student Debt Crisis". WSJ.

HOW DID WE GET HERE?

The student loan system was built in the 1960s on the over-arching belief that higher education is a safe and worthy investment for both society and the individual. At the time, the first children born after World War II—the baby boomer generation—were beginning to graduate from high school and enter college. The American economy was becoming more sophisticated and knowledge-based. Education had been a key factor behind the nation's impressive economic growth and rising living standards, to say nothing of its standing as a global superpower.

At the start of the century, less than a tenth of American workers had a high school diploma, let alone a college degree. But by the 1960s, high school was universally required, and college attendance was growing rapidly. Economists started to talk about college as an investment in human capital that drove wage gains for workers and raised the economy's total productivity.

Officials in the administration of President Lyndon B. Johnson and members of Congress wanted to make sure that everyone shared in the gains. Previously, college had largely been confined to upper-income whites. Now the hope was that colleges would level the playing field for minorities, the poor and the middle class. Banks were reluctant to make loans to students, who were viewed as risky prospects, so

Johnson successfully pushed Congress to pass the 1965 Higher Education Act, which provided funding for the government to guarantee student loans made by banks, shifting almost all the risk to taxpayers.

But Johnson wanted to come up with a longer-term strategy for financing higher education. He and Congress faced a pivotal decision: Should the bulk of federal money go to schools or directly to students? The task of settling that question fell to a young economist in the administration named Alice Rivlin.

The Rivlin panel came down on the side of direct aid to students, essentially endorsing a voucher system—the one that we have today—in which the federal government gives students a combination of loans and grants. Student loans became an entitlement, like Social Security, which students were free to spend at the school of their choice.[67]

WHAT COULD GO WRONG? AS IT TURNED OUT, A LOT

The combination of open access to schools and open access to loans turned the higher education market into a version of the Wild West. Schools of all types, banks, nonprofit guarantee agencies, and Wall Street investors competed for federal

---

67 Mitchell, Josh. 2019. "The Long Road To The Student Debt Crisis". WSJ.

student loan dollars. In particular, the system gave colleges an incentive to maximize the tuition they extracted from students and the federal taxpayer by boosting fees and enrollment, which meant relaxing admissions standards.

The voucher system, combined with a lack of government oversight, created perverse incentives: Colleges could raise money quickly by admitting academically suspect students while suffering little or no consequences if their students dropped out and defaulted on loans. The market was suddenly flooded with cheap money, which led to a surge in the ranks of college-going students. This cycle continued throughout the 1980s and 1990s, as Sallie Mae and private banks that fronted students the money for the federal student loan program made big profits—and schools collected more money.

By 2000, higher education had become an opaque and dysfunctional market. Students and families have had to accept it as an article of faith that taking on big college debt is still worth it, since official data has been hard to come by. The severe recession that began in 2007 led to a boom in college and graduate-school enrollment, as workers who couldn't find jobs went into higher education. President Barack Obama's administration tried to address many of higher education's problems through regulation. For example, it put in place rules designed to force for-profit trade schools to shut down if too many of their students defaulted on loans. But Mr. Obama doubled down on the basic idea that college is a safe investment for students and the country. In his first speech to Congress, in February 2009, he said that his budget would invest in education, in part through student loans, and asked every American to spend at least a year in college. "Every American will need to get more than a high school diploma," he said.[68]

MORE AMERICANS GAINED ACCESS TO COLLEGE

In several important ways, the student loan system has achieved the objectives set out by policy makers a half-century ago. More Americans gained access to college: The number of full-time workers with bachelor's degrees has risen from 7.6 million in 1980 to 19.5 million today. The share of Americans aged 25 and older with a bachelor's degree reached 34.2 percent in 2017, double what it was in 1980, Education Department data show. For the typical borrower, higher education is an investment that pays off: The college premium—the amount graduates earn over workers without degrees—remains at an all-time high. About 40 percent of all student debt goes to finance graduate degrees, including law and medical degrees, which typically lead to high salaries.[69]

---

68 *ibid*
69 *ibid*

But those averages obscure big problems. Many groups are benefiting unevenly, or not at all, from college degrees. "The extent of the returns depended on several demographic characteristics—most notably, when people were born and their races or ethnicities."

Federal Reserve Bank of St. Louis reported earlier this year. "In particular, the financial benefits one can expect from a college degree appear to be lower among people born in the 1980s, and they remain unequal across racial and ethnic groups."

Worse, millions of students took out loans, but never earned a degree. High college dropout rates continue. And many households and employers no longer seem to think that college is "worth it." Companies including Google, Apple, and IBM have dropped the requirement that job applicants have college degrees: They no longer think that a degree is automatically needed to succeed.

THE FAR-REACHING IMPACT OF THE STUDENT DEBT CRISIS

Student debt can destroy credit, delay marriage and children, make buying a home impossible, and turn hopes of career success and financial stability into a nightmare of struggling for decades just to catch up. It can become a vicious cycle that spills across generations: Some people in low- or modest-paying jobs are still paying off college loans even as their children rack up similar debts.

I'm personally aware of what it's like to leave Grad school already saddled with significant debt. But the mission of relieving student debt goes beyond personal for me. We must do something to diminish the impact of the student debt crisis. It is already curtailing the economic prospects of an entire generation, causing delays in achieving career goals and forcing millions of young adults to forego making charity donations and saving for retirement.

Nobody doubts that a better-educated workforce is more likely to enjoy higher earnings. But education by itself is a necessary insufficient increase-earnings tool. Yes, people absolutely need more education and skill training, but they also need an economic context wherein they can realize the economic returns from their improved education.

The student debt crisis is forcing many to put their lives on hold while they try to figure out how to pay off the debt that they had to acquire to pursue career success and their piece of the American dream.

HIGHER EDUCATION RETURN ON INVESTMENT

The Department of Education released information about how much debt students are taking on to earn degrees from various academic programs at American colleges and universities. The data shows one sector in particular with outsize debt: graduate school.

Within the graduate school sector, the fast-growing master's degree market is replete with debt levels that make little sense. An accredited university can essentially create a master's degree in anything, set whatever price it likes, start signing up students for federal loans, and market the program as "accredited."

While undergraduate student loans are limited to $31,000 for students who are financially dependent on their parents and $57,500 for those who are not, there are no hard caps on how much someone can borrow for graduate school. That means that students can borrow not merely for tuition, but also for living expenses, notoriously high in cities like San Francisco or New York. Anyone who passes a credit check is eligible to borrow the full cost of attending any accredited graduate school, regardless of how much money a person has, or doesn't have, in the bank. Borrowing for graduate school can be a sound financial decision, if the degree reliably leads to a well-paying career. But the new federal data suggests that the graduate school market often behaves in strange and erratic ways.

IS AN M.B.A. STILL WORTH IT?

While people can debate about the financial ROI of a master's degree in art or education, an MBA has always been considered as a well worth investment. For decades, an MBA was the hallmark of upward mobility towards the C-suite of top companies.

But the rapid rate of technological change, and the digitization of the workplace are chipping away the traditional graduate-level business program. To meet today's business needs, start-ups and massive companies alike are increasingly hiring technologists, developers, and engineers in place of the MBA graduates they may have preferentially hired in the past.

Looking at the Harvard Business Review's Top 100 CEOs in 2018 list, more CEOs on the list held engineering degrees than MBAs (thirty-four held engineering degrees, while thirty-two held MBAs). There's much more to leading innovative companies than an advanced business degree.[70]

The data speaks for itself: Enrollment in two-year, full-time MBA programs in the United States fell by more than one-third from 2010 to 2016. During the 2018 admissions period, applications to business schools in the

---

70 *"The Best-Performing Ceos In The World 2018". 2019. Harvard Business Review.*

United States dropped 7 percent from the previous year. Top MBA schools started seeing declines in application numbers, too.

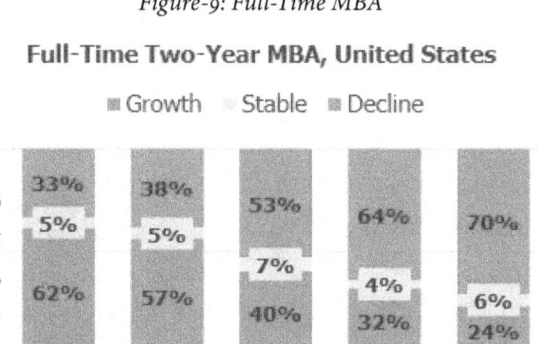

Figure-9: Full-Time MBA

Full-Time Two-Year MBA, United States

▪ Growth ▪ Stable ▪ Decline

	2014	2015	2016	2017	2018
Growth	33%	38%	53%	64%	70%
Stable	5%	5%	7%	4%	6%
Decline	62%	57%	40%	32%	24%

Percentage of programs

The odds are no longer with MBA students. The system is broken. As Dale Stevens wrote in the Wall Street Journal: "If you want a business education, the odds aren't with you, unfortunately, in business school." [71]Why? Because MBAs are, in today's working world, largely irrelevant. By the time you finish your first year, half of what you've learned will be outdated as technology moves that quickly. Books can't keep up. Old school business schools definitely can't keep up, and are also becoming ROI negative:

---

71 *Stephens, Dale. 2019. "A Smart Investor Would Skip The M.B.A.". WSJ.*

Figure-10: B School Blues

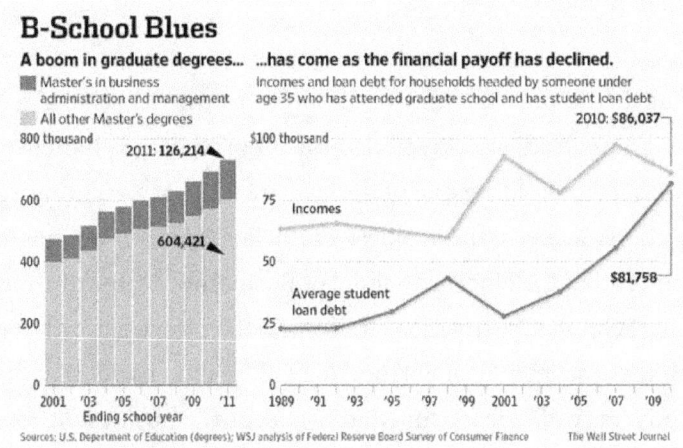

B-School Blues

A boom in graduate degrees...

Master's in business administration and management

All other Master's degrees

800 thousand

2011: 126,214

604,421

...has come as the financial payoff has declined.

Incomes and loan debt for households headed by someone under age 35 who has attended graduate school and has student loan debt

$100 thousand

2010: $86,037

Incomes

Average student loan debt

$81,758

Sources: U.S. Department of Education (degrees); WSJ analysis of Federal Reserve Board Survey of Consumer Finance   The Wall Street Journal

On the other hand, graduate schools—particularly at the upper echelon—show great numbers of unicorns they generate. Stanford's eighteen unicorn companies account for over 5 percent of global unicorns, and Harvard is responsible for producing just under 5 percent. Combined, just these two universities (out of over 5,000 in the United States, and thousands more around the world) account for one in ten of the billion-dollar private companies in the world.

It's no coincidence that some 40 percent of Silicon Valley venture capitalists are alumni of either Harvard or Stanford. Beyond prestige, the success these elite business programs see translates directly into cultivating unmatched networks and relationships. From future investors to advisors, friends, and potential business partners, relationships are critical to an entrepreneur's success.

But, while prestige may be inherent to the degree earned by graduates from these business programs, the credibility boost from holding one of these degrees is not a guaranteed path to success in the business world. For example, you might expect that the Harvard School of Business or Stanford Graduate School of Business would come out on top when tallying up the alma maters of Fortune 500 CEOs. It turns out that the University of Wisconsin-Madison leads the business school pack with fourteen CEOs to Harvard's twelve.

With the current wave of digital change, the average person changes jobs roughly twelve times in their career (and that's just averaged data—imagine the numbers for millennials and Gen Z). There's no single-degree solution that can serve you throughout your career. Your degree or MBA will help you secure your first grad job, but that's all. To keep advancing, you need to keep learning.

WILL COLLEGE AND GRADUATE PROGRAMS STILL BE RELEVANT IN THE FUTURE?

A college degree is extremely important. It's not the only route to the middle-class, but it's the most surefire route. For example, see this figure from WSJ on unemployment rates by education.

Figure-11: School Work

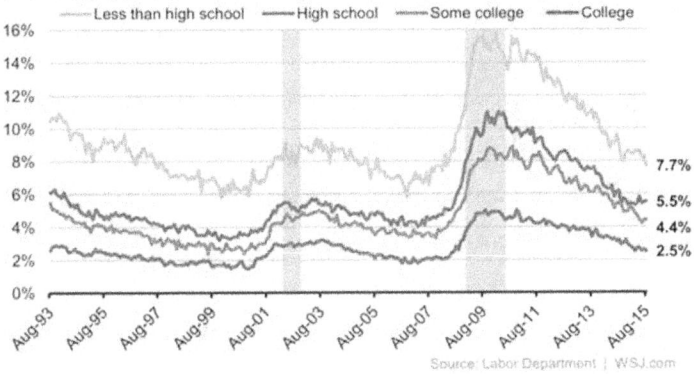

School Work
Unemployment rate for civilians 25 years and over by educational attainment, seasonally adjusted

The unemployment rate is three times as high among less than high school adults as among college graduates, and twice as high among high school only adults. The earnings differential between college and high school has doubled since 1980, and the lifetime value of a college degree net of tuition has increased by roughly $300K since the 1960s.[72]

There's every reason to think that highly-educated workers will continue to be in high demand for decades to come. Prospects are much weaker for workers without specialized skills. But it's worth noting that there are good noncollege jobs that will be around for quite some time:

---

72 Holm, Erik. 2019. *"August Jobs Report: Everything You Need To Know"*. WSJ

Yet, too often, degrees are still thought of as lifelong stamps of professional competency. They tend to create a false sense of security, perpetuating the illusion that work—and the knowledge it requires—is static. It's not.

Expect the change to keep coming. The WEF cites one estimate finding that "65 percent of children entering primary school will end up in jobs that don't yet exist."[73] These trends aren't just academic.

While my parents only had one job throughout their life, I already had several by the age of thirty-two, and my children, not only can they expect to have many jobs throughout their working lives, but multiple jobs at the same time.

It is, therefore, imperative that we encourage more options to thrive without our current overreliance on college degrees as proof of ability. We need new routes to success and hope.

THE CLASS OF 2030

What skills will today's kindergarteners need to be ready for life by the time they graduate as the class of 2030? How can technology support their educational journey?

---

73   *"Chapter 1: The Future Of Jobs And Skills". 2019. The Future Of Jobs.*

To answer these critical questions, Microsoft launched a key piece of research: "The class of 2030 and life-ready learning: The technology imperative." [74]To conduct the research, they talked with seventy thought leaders around the world, reviewed 150 pieces of existing research, and surveyed 2,000 teachers and 2,000 students across Canada, Singapore, the United Kingdom, and the United States.

They found two core themes: social emotional skills and personalized learning. Whilst not new in education, these are newly important for more people. Employers are placing a premium on social skills and emotional literacy with up to 40 percent of future jobs requiring explicit social emotional skills. Academics are noting their impact on deep learning and the students themselves recognize these skills are critical for success. The research highlighted personalized learning as an approach which supports skill development—both cognitive and social and emotional by guiding students toward greater autonomy and control.

The students were clear: they want to develop these skills to navigate their own learning—to explore and make choices that unlock their curiosity and potential and they want teachers who know and understand them as individuals.

---

74 *"Class Of 2030 || Microsoft EDU". 2019. Educationblog.Microsoft.Com.*

Three technologies were highlighted in the research as showing great promise to support social and emotional skill development and personalized learning approaches; collaborative platforms, mixed reality and analytics powered by AI. Students across the four surveyed countries prioritized a range of social-emotional and higher-order skills; notably, students valued digital skills, creativity, and problem solving higher than teachers.

While not new in education, these skills are newly important to more people and are taking center stage alongside deeper cognitive skills and content knowledge in the classroom and in the workforce. By 2030, it is predicted that between 30 to 40 percent of jobs will require explicit social-emotional skills. Personalized learning, which is a student-centered approach, emerged as one of the most promising ways to develop social-emotional and deeper cognitive skills.

* * *

The class of 2030 and future generations will face social and global problems beyond what we can imagine. They will learn and engage with each other, with technology and with information in entirely new ways. And they will enter a workforce where job functions and roles will be dramatically different from today.

Free college, online-driven education and aligning skills with in-demand jobs are just some of the ways that college may change in the future. After all, with student loan debt in the trillions, college graduates unprepared for entry-level positions and many people dropping out before earning a degree, it's become clear that something has to be done to address higher education's problems.

CHAPTER 5

THE PATH TO TRANSFORMATION IN EDUCATION

- Higher-Education Transformation

- New Models of Higher Education

- Education Should Be Like Everything Else—An On-Demand Service

- Online Learning and the Ed Tech Industry

- Boot Camp Versus College

HIGHER-EDUCATION TRANSFORMATION

AI, automation, and other innovative technologies won't only transform the way we work, but also the way we learn. Education is ripe for disruptive change leading to innovative practices that improve learning outcomes for students. What might have worked in the past will not necessarily have the same impact today, as the world has changed dramatically in a short period of time.

We are all making more use of digital technology. But many people think the "essence" of teaching (transferring knowledge, information, and skills) hasn't dramatically changed. This is a mistake. Things are already different. In a digital age, education is less about students acquiring knowledge. Instead, the classroom of the future focuses on offering an experience that builds the capacity for living and working in a world of artificial intelligence, connected machines, and automation. Such an experience can only be "successful" if it spurs curiosity, unleashes creativity, and demands teamwork.

ONLINE LEARNING EXPERIENCE

Blending the traditional and the technological—Internet will play a bigger role in learning. While the debate rages on about the need for a traditional college degree, progress will continue to be made in marrying a traditional college education with online classes.

The Internet is increasingly becoming a tool for colleges and universities around the country who see the value it can bring.

"About 50 percent of all private colleges have some kind of online program," says David L. Warren, president of the National Association of Independent Colleges and Universities. "A vast majority are blended courses that utilize online education opportunities, but the brick and mortar continue to be there."[75]

According to Warren, while the Internet will increasingly play a larger role in how college students learn, schools will maintain a tight connection between the online world and their physical campuses and communities. What's more, over time, Warren sees an increase in one-on-one learning with faculty members and the flexibility of how the courses are offered.

Still, that doesn't mean the blending of these two mediums will be easy sailing. According to Avi Flombaum, Dean of Flatiron School, the New York-based coding school, the challenge will be in making sure schools are creating programs that truly reflect how people learn. "Learning is social, and knowledge is almost always transferred from person to person," [76]says Flombaum.

---

75 Ibid
76 Ibid

"In the future, the idea of community should be built into every digital learning experience – students across the world supporting each other, content improving the more people use it. And then, that should seamlessly transition into the offline experience in the form of co-learning, similar to today's co-working spaces, where we know people thrive," Flombaum says.

SHOPPING FOR COLLEGE

Change takes time. And for higher education, there won't be a complete revolution within the next few years. However, there should be a lot of progress, whether it's in how students evaluate schools or how the student debt crisis is handled.

Take shopping for college, for starters. During the next five years, students and families are expected to become more savvy shoppers, weighing attributes that historically haven't been considered when deciding on what school to attend or what kinds of degrees to pursue. "For 300-plus years, we evaluated the quality by the square footage of the library or what exclusivity it has," says Carol D'Amico, executive vice president of National Engagement and Philanthropy with USA Funds, a nonprofit focused on increasing access to higher education. "The quality of the consumer experience has not been part of the equation."[77]

---

77 *"What Will Higher Education Look Like 5, 10 Or 20 Years From Now?". 2019. Goodcall.Com.*

Over the next five years, D'Amico sees a shift happening, where potential students will weigh college return on investment, including the outcomes of the past students, job prospects upon graduation, and the overall college experience more seriously than whether a school has a state-of-the-art gym. Similar to how people get real-person reviews of restaurants, doctors, and other services, the same diligence will be applied to shopping for college.

EMPLOYERS ARE NOT SATISFIED

For decades, colleges and universities have focused on churning out graduates that are well-rounded individuals. But increasingly they are dropping the ball when it comes to giving employers graduates with the skills needed to succeed. That has prompted employers to spend money training their new hires—or looking outside the pool of college graduates for qualified workers.

As a result, in the next few years, experts expect colleges and universities to be more accountable to what they are teaching their students. There will be greater collaboration with corporations to ensure students are gaining the correct skills for the in-demand jobs. There will always be a time and place to analyze Thoreau, but a lot of focus will also be placed on communications and technical skills.

"Employers are finally signaling that what they are getting is just not good enough," says D'Amico of USA Funds. "Only about 11 percent of employers think that higher education is doing a good job." [78]According to D'Amico, there are an increasing number of start-ups that are emerging to close the gap between what employers say they want from graduates and what they are getting from the experience.

Whether or not in twenty years' time we will get to the point where college is free or debt-free is still up for debate. But it is clear that if we do nothing, tough times are ahead—not only for college students, but the nation at large.

EDUCATION SHOULD BE LIKE EVERYTHING ELSE—AN ON-DEMAND SERVICE

Today's students order a Lyft when they want to go from point A to point B, rather than waiting for a cab. They stream shows on Netflix and songs on Spotify, rather than wait for the next episode to air or their favorite song to come on the radio. Today's students are living in a system that is different from the one I grew up in—and our educational system hasn't caught up.

The fact is, 44 percent of recent college graduates between the ages of twenty-two and twenty-seven work in jobs that do not require a college degree. Few course curricula reflect the

---

78 *"What Will Higher Education Look Like 5, 10 Or 20 Years From Now?". 2019. Goodcall.Com.*

current trends in technology. Traditional college programs are rigid and confining. For the 73 percent of students who work while in college, attending class five days a week at a specific time is challenging, if not impossible.[79]

Figure-12: Education System

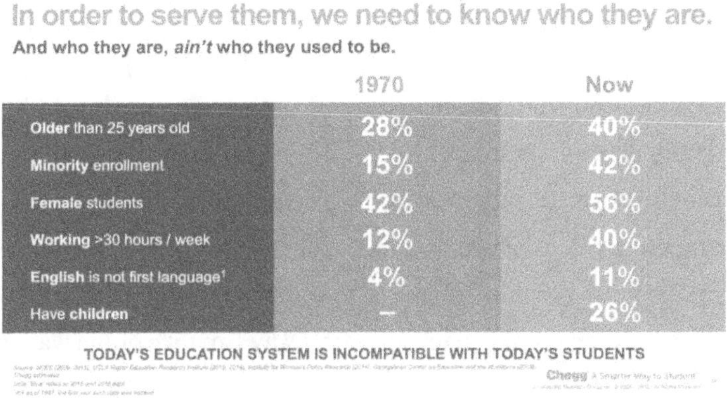

In order to serve them, we need to know who they are.
And who they are, *ain't* who they used to be.

	1970	Now
Older than 25 years old	28%	40%
Minority enrollment	15%	42%
Female students	42%	56%
Working >30 hours / week	12%	40%
English is not first language[1]	4%	11%
Have children	—	26%

TODAY'S EDUCATION SYSTEM IS INCOMPATIBLE WITH TODAY'S STUDENTS

Chegg A Smarter Way to Student

Students aren't studying in the afternoons after class or on weekends; the typical student's primary learning time is 9:00 p.m. While student's primary way to access material is on their phones or mobile devices, many professors still prohibit students from using these devices in the classroom.

Simply put, today's educational system is incompatible with the needs of the modern student.

---

79 *"Education Should Be Like Everything Else. An On-Demand Service". 2019. World Economic Forum.*

Most students go to college to become a positive contributor to society and an active participant in life. But we're letting them down. We are expecting students to go to a particular place at a particular time to learn. This is in an age when everything in their lives, such as entertainment, transport, and food, comes to them at any time of day.

Rather than telling students to borrow the money and hope there's a job that will help pay off their debt, we should be using technology to both reduce their costs and to accelerate the time from learning to earning with on-demand education and curricula that prepare them for the jobs of the future. In many ways, the idea of going to a certain place at a certain time to learn seems anachronistic. Why can't we binge watch our education?

FUTURE TRENDS

Three trends will shape the higher education world in the next five years says Dr. Guvin Suss:

1. Interdisciplinary programs: Programs that combines more than one branch of knowledge. For example: creativeness and economy, or data and philosophy.

2. Focus on developing creativity: 25 to 30 percent of the program will be based on teaching creativeness and innovation.

3. Hybrid programs: Programs that are strongly connected to the industry and industry trends.

Suss believes that in an era where every student has a computer attached to his body (e.g., smartphone) the academy has to provide students a unique set of tools that will help them become more creative.

"Today information is abundance, so educational institutions should focus more on developing skills like creativity, communication and strategic thinking." Says Prashant Malaviya, Senior Associate Dean of MBA Programs at Georgetown University.

Dean Malaviya talks about a new model for higher education that will emerge in the future and includes four layers of education:

- Knowledge: Fundamental knowledge that every student has to learn.

- Skills: Certain set of skills that students will choose to learn according to their future goals.

- Capabilities: Critical thinking, for example, understand how to work with machines and how algorithms work.

- Creating Mind-Set: Teach people how to think, in an unbiased way. We tend to teach students knowledge in silos, meaning instead of giving them a cross functional education we are focused more on educating them separately on the different aspects of the business, and in real life, an ability to think, act, and communicate with cross functional teams is very important.

According to Malaviya's prediction, schools will either go online (more relevant for community colleges, and small universities), and teach knowledge and skills—the first two layers in the education model, or they will focus on the capabilities and mind-set (the last two layers), which at the moment students prefer to learn them offline.

The huge cost for entering the online world, is a big barrier for institutions that don't have big pockets according to Malaviya.

"I believe that higher-education institutions will eventually outsource the Skills education. I think the companies themselves and the HR departments will be responsible for teaching their employees the right skills for the job, while the universities will be a place to learn strategy and executive education. We will also see more segmented degrees where each business school will have a portfolio of degrees design to answer market needs in terms of knowledge and flexibility."

In regard to the future of business schools, Malaviya doesn't see them disappear anytime soon, "Business schools teach students business fundamentals, like accounting, operation, marketing and finance. Business managers will always have to know it and have these skills, so I don't worry whether a machine will replace those needs anytime soon."

"The future of education will be about data and personalization."

Malaviya envisions a dashboard with functional metrics and information on each student in class, including a scale of one to one hundred to measure student performance and progress in each class.

In addition to a sophisticated metrics to measure how much progress each student has made developing his Soft Skills, such as: teamwork, global mind-set, and leadership.

Prashant concludes that we are to determine how AI and other disruptive technologies will impact our lives, and it's our responsibility to design a new policy in a way that doesn't cause too many people to lose their jobs.

NEW MODELS OF HIGHER-EDUCATION

ONLINE LEARNING AND THE ED TECH INDUSTRY

At a time when a traditional college education has never been more expensive, online courses have never been more popular, with fourteen consecutive years of enrollment growth. At a time when two-thirds of teachers say they're stressed out—almost twice the rate of the general working population—entrepreneurs are pumping out digitally native lessons and courseware.

Thanks to online learning platforms, a physical classroom is no longer the only place to gain an education. You can now learn anything, anywhere. The democratization of education has helped break down traditional barriers of access like high costs and location, resulting in a more skilled and informed workplace and citizenry.

These days, there are countless types of classes and online learning platforms to choose from. You could spend years absorbing the differences in coding languages, strategizing how to most effectively leverage email marketing tactics for your small business, or in a very meta twist, learning how to learn—and then move on to a different platform and do it all over again.

"Learn Anything, On Your Schedule"

Take Udemy for example—the world's largest marketplace for online learning, offering over 55,000 courses across a large range of categories. Its mission is "to improve lives through learning." Their Course categories range from IT and software to Lifestyle and Personal Development.

And the pricing ranges from $10 to $200 per course.

On February 12, 2016, Udemy announced that more than 10 million students have taken one of its courses. In the United States, there were about 13 million students working toward a four-year degree during fall 2015 semester, according to the Department of Education. It is another example of the rising popularity of online education.

Some observers have floated online education as a cheaper alternative to traditional four-year degrees. But Udemy CEO Dennis Yang, believes online education can serve a different role, helping professionals long out of college keep up with changing workplaces. "Through a combination of technology, automation and globalization, things are changing quickly, but at the same time, what we learn in school, and how we're teaching and being taught in school, is the same,"[80] says Yang. "So traditional education is not really keeping up from a pace standpoint."

---

80 *"Udemy Thinks It's Cracked The Future Of Online Education".*
2019. Time.

Udemy courses can be rewarding for the platform's instructors, too. Rob Percival, a former high school teacher in the United Kingdom, has made $6.8 million from a Udemy web development course that took him three months to build. "It got to the stage several months ago where I hit a million hours of viewing that particular month," he says. "It's a very different experience than the classroom. The amount of good you can do on this scale is staggering. It's a fantastic feeling knowing that it's out there, and while I sleep people can still learn from me."

To be sure, Percival is an outlier. His course happens to be Udemy's most viewed offering. But the promise of monetizing their knowledge and experience remains an attractive lure even for instructors who don't turn to Udemy for their full-time income. More than 20,000 people have uploaded a course to the site.

The success of programs like Udemy, General Assembly, and The Flatiron School in New York City lead to an inevitable question, at least if you're technically inclined: Why spend $200,000 on four years of college when you can spend $10,000 on 12 weeks of training and get hired by an app developer for $70,000 or more?

BOOT CAMP VERSUS COLLEGE

Two viable paths to getting a job in tech—boot camp and college—have very different costs, timeframes, and overall outcomes. To decide between the two, you should first ask yourself what kind of educational experience you want to have. College has traditionally been the place young adults become informed, intelligent citizens, emerging with skills considered transferable to most work environments. While a majority of students and employers still accept this philosophy, the longer, more general program may not appeal to everyone.

As has been the norm for years, students working towards a degree in computer science will often spend four years earning their degree in a traditional environment. Graduating with a computer science degree, therefore, can mean that students have taken a generalized course of study that covers overall principles of technology and may also give students a sampling of harder programming skills.

Boot camps teach both hard and soft skills in a fraction of the time, often twelve to fifteen weeks. The programs offer hands-on training in practical coding as well as workplace communication skills and real-world problem solving. Because boot camps are shorter, they are more adaptable and can change to match the needs of the job market. The very nature of college's set schedule and pace may not work for all learners. College is not always the right (or viable) option for everyone, which makes the flexibility of boot camps an attractive alternative to an ever-growing pool of employers.

There has been an explosion in the number of so-called "coding boot camps" over the last decade. The premise is simple: students pay to enroll and are given a crash course in computer programming using the most common languages and tools in the industry. Courses typically last six months to a year, and those that perform well have a good chance of landing a well-paid job at a technology company, without having to spend the time and money required to go through a university degree. The cost of enrolling in a coding boot camp is still high, however, according to Course Report, boot camp tuition fees can range from $9,000 to $21,000. This is still not as expensive and time-consuming as college, given that many offer their tuition online, but it is still expensive enough for it to be considered a life decision for many to enroll.

"Learn to Code, Pay Nothing Upfront"

One of the highest profile coding boot camps is Lambda School, a San Francisco based boot camp offering courses in computer science combined with either full-stack Web, Android, or iOS development. Students can also take courses in Data Science or UX Design. These are all highly in-demand skills in the technology industry. Entry level positions in these roles in tech-centric US cities such as San Francisco and New York City can net six-figure starting salaries. This boot camp model seems to be working: Lambda School announced in January that it raised $30 million in Series B funding from venture capital firms such as Google Ventures, and renowned startup incubator Y Combinator amongst others, giving it a post-money valuation of around $150 million.[81]

In addition to having no physical campus with courses being delivered online, Lambda School is offering an extremely attractive financial arrangement for those that enroll: as an alternative to paying the $20,000 tuition fee up front, students can opt to enter an income share agreement. This allows them to defer payment until they are earning over $50,000 annually for two years. At that point, 17 percent of their salary is paid back to Lambda School until the debt is paid off. If students are unable to find a job with this level of compensation after five years, they owe nothing. For students from disadvantaged backgrounds, or those wanting to make a complete career switch, this offer is seriously enticing

Boot camps are trendy in part because their compressed curricula and focus on job placement in high-demand fields are catnip for higher education reformers and policy makers who feel traditional colleges are failing to prepare graduates for jobs.

Yet, boot camps typically cater to bachelor's degree holders who can afford to spend about $12,000 on a twelve-week coding program. While many in the industry describe their role

---

81   "Coding Bootcamps: A Glimpse At The Future Of Education?". 2019. Medium.

as being an add-on to a college education, not a replacement, boot camps could encroach on the turf of graduate schools, particularly if short-term credentials become more popular.

GO PRO EARLY

"Instead of going to college to get a job, students will increasingly be going to a job to get a college degree." [82]Says Brandon Busteed, President of Kaplan University Partners

What does this mean exactly?

Today, the number one reason why Americans value and pursue higher education is "to get a good job." The path has always been assumed as linear: first, go to college and then, get a good job. But what if there was a path to get a good job first—a job that comes with a college degree?

According to Busteed, in the near future, a substantial number of students (including many of the most talented) will go straight to work for employers that offer a good job along with a college degree and ultimately a path to a great career.

Higher education won't be eliminated from the model; "degrees and other credentials will remain valuable and

---

82 *"This Will Be The Biggest Disruption In Higher Education".*
    2019. Forbes.Com.

desired, but for a growing number of young people they'll be part of getting a job as opposed to college as its own discrete experience. This is already happening in the case of working adults and employers that offer college education as a benefit. But it will soon be true among traditional age students."

A Kaplan University Partners-QuestResearch study predicts that "as many as one-third of all traditional students in the next decade will "Go Pro Early" in work directly out of high school with the chance to earn a college degree as part of the package."[83]

When asked about a potential new pathway for their children to get a college degree, 74% of all parents of K-12 students would consider a route where their child would be hired directly out of high school by an employer that offers a college degree while working.

A 'Go Pro Early' model is certainly not for everyone, though. The study identified two types of students for which it is most suited and appealing: those who are "ambitious and debt averse" and those who are "college hesitant and debt averse." The first group represents students who already have a career in mind, who value work experience, and their families are looking for ways to make college more affordable. The second

---

83   *"Exploring New Routes To Success - Kaplan". 2019. Kaplan.*

group represents families who are also looking for more affordable college options, but for students who don't find college to be a perfect fit for them, prefer an applied learning environment and are considering trade school options too.

Top employers such as Price Waterhouse Coopers (PwC) are already offering these kinds of opportunities where students can go straight from high school into apprenticeship programs that weave credentials and degrees into the process. And more broadly, there is a growing trend among large employers to offer college degrees as an employee benefit to attract and retain better talent and up-skill their existing workforce. Examples include: Walmart, Discover, Starbucks, Disney, Papa John's and many others.

Busteed believes that this trend will soon lead to more employers not only offering college degrees as a benefit for current employees but increasingly as a powerful recruiting tool to hire top talent directly out of high school as well. As the war for talent continues to intensify among employers, it will inevitably lead them to find that talent earlier and accelerate talent development in new ways.

"It's simply a matter of time before the new world of *going to a job to get a college degree* disrupts the linear higher education pathway as we know it." According to Busteed.

CHAPTER 6

THE FUTURE OF LEARNING— TECHNOLOGY TRENDS IN EDUCATION

- Emerging Technologies to Enhance Teaching and Learning: AI, VR, AR, and Mobile

- Cloud Computing and Education

- Personalized Learning: Adaptive, Individual, Differentiated, and Competence-Based

- Learning Analytics

The education market is set for digital disruption like never before. Four trends are shaping up what will collectively change how students learn and teachers teach. There are countless new players entering the classroom, from Soul Machines; AI teacher specializing in energy use and sustainability to smart "lab schools" with personalized curricula. Given the fact that our educational system hasn't changed in many decades (perhaps a century), it's time to rethink our education, during this transformative era of technology.

EMERGING TECHNOLOGIES TO ENHANCE TEACHING AND LEARNING: AI, VR, AR, AND MOBILE

ARTIFICIAL INTELLIGENCE

With AI, every aspect of the traditional learning environment is up for reimagining. Will the classroom continue to be a physical space? Or instead, will it be a virtual "space" using networked augmented or virtual reality technologies?

As AI applications accelerate across many sectors, it is vital that we reimagine our educational institutions for a world where AI will be ubiquitous, and students need a different kind of training than they currently get. Right now, many students do not receive instruction in the kinds of skills that will be needed in an AI-dominated landscape. For example, the shortages of data scientists, computer scientists, engineers, coders, and platform developers. Unless our educational system generates more people with these capabilities, it will limit AI development.

Because educational institutions have continued to rely on traditional lecture/classroom settings in recent years, they oversaw unconceivable potential from AI solutions to complement traditional learning by improving current common practices and unburdening teachers. Here are four areas where AI will transform education in the near future:

1. *AI tutors and gamification*: Game-based learning or gamification applies the elements and design techniques of gaming to nongame problems, like education. By making learning fun, it inspires students to learn not just while they're in school, but throughout their lives. Examples include Kahoot, an app that lets teachers create tests, quizzes, and surveys that can be incorporated into online games played by students. Tanah, an app developed by UNESCO, the Red Cross and others, makes a game out of disaster preparedness, helping people learn how to survive a tsunami or quake.

2. *Automated grading:* AI technologists are working on solutions to automate the tedious grading process, and one successful example is the AI-based grading solution

Gradescope, a system which is already used in many universities including Berkeley and Stanford University. Gradescope asks teachers to scan the students' handwritten test solutions and automatically applies predefined grading criteria to all tests, thereby reducing grading time significantly and providing a transparent grading key to students.

3. *24/7 personal student and teacher support/chatbot:* Professor Goel from Georgia Institute of Technology introduced a new teaching assistant, Jill Watson, to his class. Ms. Watson replied to questions, sent out reminders for due dates, and asked questions in the middle of the week to trigger discussions. Students described her responses as reliable and her tone as colloquial. The only difference to an ordinary teaching assistant was that Ms. Watson was not a real person, but an AI bot developed to reduce the workload of professor Goel's PhD students. Ms. Watson took over tasks in which she was at least 97 percent confident that she knew the right answer[84]. Such an AI-based bot is helpful for both teachers because it reduces their overall workload and students because they can get help on common problems instantly and around the clock.

---

84 *Hill, David. 2019. "AI Teaching Assistant Helped Students Online— And No One Knew The Difference". Singularity Hub.*

4. *Improve education to fight poverty:* Poverty and lack of education are highly linked; AI can help impact education levels in poorer areas. We could soon see intelligent chatbots being able to stand in as teachers for students without access to other forms of schooling. As long as there is access to a computer/internet connection, an AI-teacher could guide students through a syllabus using real-time analytics and machine learning to assess the education and learning level and skills of individual students. This could entirely eradicate the money-barrier and inequality that so many people across the world come up against in education.

In most developing countries, schools lack experienced teachers and resources to enhance students' knowledge. As a result, many students still have to walk long distances to get to the nearest school, which has created education gaps, especially in rural areas. AI tools such as personalized learning assistants can simplify learning by making tutoring services and learning materials accessible to all students, wherever they are. This would allow students to learn at anytime from anywhere. With AI, education is made easy and accessible to more people.

AR\VR:

Augmented reality (AR) is a technology that superimposes a computer-generated image on a user's view of the real world, thus providing a composite view. AR in education will soon affect the conventional learning process and has the potential to change the location and timing of studying to introduce new and additional ways and methods. Educators know that the learning process should be all about creativity and inter-action. While teachers do not necessarily need to recruit all students into science, their goal is to get them interested in a subject. That's where AR could come in handy. Nowadays, approximately 90 percent of young people own smartphones. Most of them are active smartphone users that use these gadgets to access social platforms, play games, and to be in connection with friends and relatives. The potential of combining smartphones and augmented reality for educa-tion is big, though it still has to be fully discovered. AR, in various ways, could grant students extra digital informa-tion about any subject, and make complex information easier to understand.

AR technology has an ability to render objects that are hard to imagine and turn them into 3D models, thus making it easier to grasp the abstract and difficult content. This is especially good for visual learners and practically anyone to translate theoretical material into a real concept. For exam-ple, Polytechnic Institute of Leiria in Portugal integrates AR into math lessons and students report it as helpful, easy, and interesting.

MOBILE LEARNING

With the development of mobile wireless networks which improved its communication equipment, Mobile Learning came into existence and became a popular way of learning. Mobile learning (m-learning) has many advantages in terms of interactivity, portability, easy operating, and targeted users, which attracted many learners.

M-learning can definitely be touted as the next big revolutionary model in education. Ubiquitous, contextual, collaborative, and personalized in its scope, more and more students will be able to gain access to quality education through it.

Mobile learning enables students to learn whatever interests them from wherever they want to, regardless of all limitations. Previously deemed as elements that create distraction amongst students, these pocket-sized devices are now emerging as the "Mecca of learning." While e-learning has existed for a while now, and students have been turning to learning via desktops and computers, it is mobile phones that are sparking a true revolution.

CLOUD COMPUTING AND EDUCATION

Educational institutions are increasingly using the Cloud (the term "cloud" in the simplest terms means storing and accessing data and programs over the Internet instead of your computer's hard drive. The cloud is just a metaphor for the Internet) to transform the efficiency, effectiveness, and responsiveness of our schools both around the country and across the world. The ultimate goal of education is to help students grow and succeed, both in the classroom and in the workforce. The cloud can serve as a force multiplier in achieving this goal, putting additional tools to enhance student learning directly into the hands of educators.

The cloud allows schools to reallocate their limited resources towards teaching and learning. Through its pay-as-you-go model, the cloud offers flexibility and agility to scale up during peak times—like back-to-school season and end-of-grading periods—and scale down over breaks when server needs are low.

Cloud technology is also saving another invaluable resource—teachers' time. By creating access to new lesson planning resources, better identifying which interventions are working best and even grading papers, the cloud is making it possible to save precious hours every week.

The "as a service" model replaces big capital investments like software and equipment, which organizations previously needed to buy and maintain, with capabilities provided on demand over the networks.

In an educational context, "Education as a Service" (EaaS) means that students and institutions are increasingly able to follow specific areas of study, unbundled from complete programs and degrees. Educational thought leaders are admonishing institutions of higher learning to embrace EaaS as a delivery model to meet the needs of today's students.

EaaS is personalized because each student has access to areas of learning of greatest relevance to them and can pursue them at their own pace. It's affordable because it's priced according to individual courses and levels of subject matter, not an entire program or degree curriculum. It's scalable because, like software delivered through the cloud, organizations can rapidly extend access across groups, geographies and classifications as needed, just by turning on more capacity.

As with technology as a service, the advantages of this approach are personalization, affordability, and rapid scalability.

PERSONALIZED LEARNING: ADAPTIVE, INDIVIDUAL, DIFFERENTIATED, AND COMPETENCE-BASED

Personalized Learning refers to instruction in which the pace of learning and the instructional approach are optimized for the needs of each learner. Learning objectives, instructional approaches, and instructional content (and its sequencing) may all vary based on learner needs. In addition, in personalized learning, learning activities are made available that are meaningful and relevant to learners, driven by their interests and often self-initiated.

Rochelle, head of product management at Google, expects that AI applications will soon personalize the learning experience of students by suggesting individual learning objectives, selecting instructional approaches, and displaying exercises that are based on the interests and skill level of every student. Just like Netflix shows us the film that we could also like, or Spotify creates a personal playlist based on our historical music choice, AI could suggest to students their most suitable educational setting. The provision of an individual learning journey would allow students not only to learn at their own pace, but also regain the enjoyment and excitement that excellent education offers.

THERE ARE FEW KEY APPROACHES TOWARD PERSONALIZED LEARNING:[85]

- *Adaptive learning:* technology used to assign human or digital resources to learners based on their unique needs.

---

85 *"What Is Personalized Learning?". 2019. Medium.*

- *Individualized learning:* the pace of learning is adjusted to meet the needs of individual students.

- *Differentiated learning:* the approach to learning is adjusted to meet the needs of individual students.

- *Competence-based learning:* learners advance through a learning pathway based on their ability to demonstrate competency, including the application and creation of knowledge along with skills and dispositions.

Our current education system is based on grouping students merely by age, disregarding the differences in students' learning paces, interests, and talents. Consequently, in every classroom there are a few students who become bored because they have understood a subject very fast and others who are discouraged quickly because they cannot follow the teacher's explanations. In other words, education has moved towards a one size fits all solution.

A subcategory of the personalization in education is the Autonomous Learning. Take for example one of the most talked about technologies in today's world; the Self-Driving car. Just think of the possibilities a driverless car presents: reading the newspaper on the way to work, getting your workout on the exercise machine installed in the car, watching the news on TV, and the list goes on and on. Could this be our future? Some say, "Why do we need a self-driving car? My car gets me where I want to go." Future-ready thinkers say, "Why not?"

We are presented with the same kind of thinking when it comes to education. Let's think about the self-driving student, also known as the self-directed learner or the autonomous learner. What do I mean by autonomous learning?

Betts and Knapp (1981) define autonomous learning as "one who solves problems or develops new ideas through a combination of divergent and convergent thinking and functions with minimal external guidance in selected areas of endeavor." [86]Kember refers to autonomous learning as student-centered learning, shifting the focus of education from teaching to learning.

Educators have been talking about independent learning, personalized learning, and student-centered learning for a very long time. The difference today is that new technologies have given us the unique abilities to accomplish this task with greater success.

Consider the teacher the GPS of the autonomous learner. The teacher will offer up a variety of paths to students'

---

86 *"The Autonomous Learner Model For Developing Potential".*
    2019. Uncw.Edu. https://uncw.edu/ed/aig/documents/2017/
    autonomous learner model.pdf.

destinations and also suggest best routes. The teacher will be the director of the system, helping students decide on their destinations and helping them get there by passing through various necessary skills and standards that the students will need once they reach that point.

LEARNING ANALYTICS

Learning analytics is where big data meets traditional quantitative methods in education. Governments, universities, testing organizations, and massive open online course providers are collecting data about learners and how they learn. All that data, however, has been mostly untapped until the fairly recent development of the methods and tools to do so.

Learning analytics and educational data mining are the tools to transform this data into knowledge and lead, in the end, to improved education. A growing number of institutions, faculty, and administrators now see the value of better leveraging the enormous and continuously mounting collection of data from their learning management system (LMS). This data often sits unused on servers and databases, while it has the potential to advance a range of practical and theoretical needs for a variety of potential stakeholders.

Learning analytics, as well as related concepts such as academic analytics, educational data mining, and so on, explores the relationship between learning system usage with a range of outcomes that can positively impact students, faculty, administrators, researchers, and learning system designers.

BENEFITS TO STUDENTS

Analytics related to online education programs have the potential to provide students with more detailed information about their performance. For instance, learning analytics can help students see and reflect on their behavior in constructive ways to help them manage their progress toward their learning goals. Similar to a "Fitbit" or an "Apple Watch," a student-directed analytics framework has the potential to help students monitor their behavioral patterns, track changes over time, and compare their progress toward learning goals against both absolute and normative standards based on peer data.

A student with access to strong learning analytics data should be able to ask and answer:

What am I doing?

How am I doing relative to my own expectations?

How am I doing relative to faculty expectations?

How am I doing relative to my peers?

BENEFITS TO INSTRUCTORS

By utilizing learning analytics data, faculty can better monitor students and understand how course resources are being used. Some of the more obvious questions instructors ask and may find answers to via analytics include:

How are students doing in my class? Are any at risk?

What resources are they using the most?

Who is using the resources I've made available to help them?

Analytics will allow instructors to reflect on their own performance and seek better evidence for guiding instructional improvement.

BENEFITS TO ADMINISTRATORS

Learning analytics allows program directors, or other administrators, to more easily see how well their program is performing. In addition to the potential need to drill down into specific faculty, students, and course-level data, learning analytics can allow for meaningful comparisons across courses.

Learning analytics can help administrators answer questions such as:

Which courses are students finding the most engaging?

Where are "hot spots" that need attention where learning outcomes are weak, or engagement is low?

Are there student characteristics or engagement patterns that are associated with program retention?

Some of these are tricky, and like other questions raised, may require that different systems talk to each other to be able to answer important questions.

* * *

The education field looms on the horizon of positive disruption. New technologies promise to make it easier and faster for students to learn. While the direction of EdTech is unclear, analysts forecast that this promising field is in its very early beginnings.

No doubt, all education will continue to be valuable and necessary. Students and people will need to continue to adapt to technology, continue to want to learn, and continue to stay motivated in their own self-development.

I believe that the future of technology in education is about adapting to the fast-changing world, giving students an opportunity to choose their own way of learning, combining theory and practice, always taking into account the current demand of the market.

CHAPTER 7

TIME FOR A NEW RELATIONSHIP BETWEEN LEARNING AND WORK

———

- The Link Between Education and Employment

- Skills, Not Job Titles, Are the New Metric for the Labor Market

- Building Relationships Between Employers and Universities

- How LinkedIn Is Connecting Learning with Employment

- The Adaptive Learning Organization

THE LINK BETWEEN EDUCATION AND EMPLOYMENT

Over the past half century, we've been incredibly effective at treating school and college as distinct elements from work and a career. Nothing is more indicative of this trend than our belief, inherent in the system we've designed, that the best human development arises from being in school for thirteen to seventeen years and then going to work for the next forty-five years or so. This belief, and the system that perpetuates it, has probably never worked very well. It's entirely broken in today's globally competitive and rapidly changing marketplace.

Right now, in the United States, there are more jobs open than people looking for work. So, why aren't we at 100 percent employment? Why do we see fresh reports suggesting that 40 percent or more of recent college graduates are under-employed or unemployed? There are a number of answers, including the decreasing mobility of the U.S. population; a misalignment between what's being taught in school and what's needed in the workplace; and marketplace dynamics where fast-growing jobs are outpacing our ability to train people for them. All of these factors point to a skills gap of one kind or another.

This situation will require retraining and "upskilling" existing talent and reengineering our current educational model to better prepare students for workplace success. This is not a one-time effort, but should be thought of as an ongoing, lifelong process. The remaking of existing talent will require much closer partnerships between education providers and employers, which will give rise to new models where employers become educators themselves (Amazon's recent $700-million investment in talent development, almost entirely run by internal training in the company, is a good example). And our current education model will need to become substantially more applied and work integrated.

There's a pile of evidence about the most effective "education." Summarized, it points to relationship-rich and work-integrated learning experiences. The most important aspects include working on long-term projects that take a semester or more to complete and having a job or internship where you can apply what you are learning in the classroom. Both experiences double the odds that graduates will be engaged and successful in their work later.

WHAT MIGHT A MERGER OF EDUCATION AND WORK LOOK LIKE?

Co-ops and "credegrees". Co-ops are typically semester-long work experiences pedagogically tied to the course of study in most cases. Credegrees refers to the combination of a bachelor's degree with an industry-recognized credential or skill.

Liberal arts degrees will continue to thrive—but only in combination with work-related experiences and when blended with industry-relevant skills training. An art history major with a cybersecurity designation or data-science proficiency will be a white-hot graduate in the marketplace.

Employers Education and Training. Employers will shift from being passive consumers of education (simply hiring graduates) to making education and training a core strategy of their success. This will include much more active and employer-designed partnerships with educational institutions. There will also be examples of employer-designed universities—created from the ground up to serve the critical upskilling needs of a large employer's workforce. If educational institutions and accreditors aren't fast to evolve on this front, there will certainly be more examples where employers effectively replace educational institutions by creating their own fully operated education and training functions.

A "Go Pro Early" Model. The model, as discussed in the previous chapter, will become a very attractive pathway for both students and employers to enable hiring of highly talented students, directly out of high school, into full-time job and career tracks where a college degree is part of the package. In other words, instead of going to college to get a job, more people will seek a job to go to college.

* * *

The lines between human capital management, corporate training, and universities are blurring. According to a research by Deloitte, 70 percent of millennial said they believe they may only have some or few of the skills that will be required. Most said that employers are primarily responsible for training workers to meet evolving challenges; Gen Z respondents, however, said the responsibility rests with educators. "This presents an interesting opportunity for business and academia to increasingly collaborate to solve tomorrow's workforce challenges," Deloitte said in announcing its findings.[87]

To bridge this gap, educational institutions will increasingly move toward applied and work-integrated models of learning. Employers will increasingly weave learning and retraining into the fabric of the workplace.

UNIVERSITIES SHOULD BE PREPARING STUDENTS FOR THE GIG ECONOMY

How well do universities prepare students to work independently in the Gig Economy? Today's graduates are joining a workforce where the Gig Economy — including consultants,

---

87 *"2018 Deloitte Millennial Survey". 2019.*

independent contractors, freelancers, side giggers, and on-demand workers — makes up an estimated 30-40% of the U.S. workforce. [88]They're also facing an economy in which alternative work arrangements are growing faster than traditional full-time jobs and are only projected to keep growing. The recent news that the majority of Google's workforce is made up of independent and temporary workers rather than full-time employees is just one example of the rapid transformation of the corporate workforce.

Despite these changes in how we work, universities have yet to integrate the study or practice of the Gig Economy into their curriculum or career services. Instead, they continue to educate and prepare students to become full-time employees in full-time jobs. That approach does a disservice to students who will graduate ill-equipped and unprepared to succeed as independent workers. Diane Mulcahy, the author of *The Gig Economy*, describes how universities should better prepare their students for the workforce they'll enter when they graduate:

1. *Teach the Basic Skills to Work Independently.* How to create a business entity, how to manage a small back office, how to negotiate prices and consulting contracts, and how to develop and execute a marketing and

---

88 *"Universities Should Be Preparing Students For The Gig Economy".* *2019. Harvard Business Review.*

branding strategy. These basic business school skills can be re-framed to prepare students to work independently and entrepreneurially to build a portfolio of gigs.

2. *Expand Career Services to Offer Gigs.* University career services focus on matching students with full-time jobs and, so far, have ignored the rising incidence, and importance, of independent work in the Gig Economy. They are trapped in the mindset of thinking that work experience equals a full-time job and have little on offer to help students create a portfolio of work during the summer, or to help them take on side gigs during the academic year. Career Services must do a better job of helping students find work, not just jobs.

3. *Teach What They Practice.* It's paradoxical that universities are active and enthusiastic participants in the Gig Economy, yet only prepare their students to work as traditional employees in full-time jobs. Universities need only turn the mirror on themselves to see the work world their students must be ready to enter. Their own business models and practices are a case study about how employers are changing work and their workforce.

The Gig Economy is disrupting the way companies work, and the way they hire. Corporate leaders are increasingly choosing to work with independent contractors, consultants, and freelancer as needed, rather than creating full-time jobs filled with full-time employees. To succeed, students need to learn how to be self-employed, entrepreneurial, and how to run a small business, because increasingly, that's what each of us is and will do for at least some part of our careers. By teaching their students what they themselves already practice, universities can do a much better job preparing their graduates for the increasingly independent workforce of today, not the traditional jobs of yesterday.

SKILLS, NOT JOB TITLES, ARE THE NEW METRIC FOR THE LABOR MARKET

"Skills are the new currency on the labor market." [89]According to the WEF. Skills indicate demand and supply at a more nuanced level than occupations, whose required expertise and skills are changing increasingly quickly, and degrees, which are often already outdated by the time they are obtained. The current pace of change requires following the direction of a skills-based, rather than degree-based labor market, which is a much more dynamic variable. Using skills as a variable of analysis provides a powerful tool in helping policymakers prepare for the future while building resilience in the present day.

---

89 *"Skills, Not Job Titles, Are The New Metric For The Labour Market".*
2019. World Economic Forum.

THE EMERGING ROLE OF NONTRADITIONAL
CREDENTIALS—FASTER, CHEAPER ALTERNATIVES

Digital badges, verified certificates, and alternative credentials have the potential to significantly transform the relationship between higher education and businesses by providing better evidence of both "soft" and "hard" skills.

The question of whether alternative credentials—in the form of everything from badges to nanodegrees and from micro masters to certificates—will displace degrees from colleges and universities is heating up. More and more people are finding new ways outside of traditional postsecondary degree programs to show employers they possess the skills and knowledge needed for a constantly changing workplace.

Digital badges are a means of validating discrete skills and competencies acquired in any number of learning environments without having to complete a full class or program. Verified certificates are a newer development.[90] These certificates ensure that a student enrolled in a completely online course, particularly a massive open online course (MOOC) being taken by thousands of students, is the same person completing the work. Verified certificates are offered currently by two MOOC platforms: Coursera's Signature Track

---

90 *Ibid*

and edX's Verified Certificates. To earn one of these certificates, students must complete course requirements (as determined by the course creator) and pay for a process to verify their identity.

Technology is one reason behind the surge in certificates. One study found that nearly three-quarters of executive education students would consider obtaining a "micro-credential," and 63 percent may work toward a qualification that provides a "digital badge." "Nowadays, there is a growing awareness that to succeed professionally it is important to have a life-long learning mentality, and to be constantly looking to keep up to date on the latest trends," says Ana Vera, IESE's director of focused programs. Online credentials are a clever way to do this, since you do not need to quit your job or forgo a salary.

While I was an MBA student, I participated in such programs myself. I decided that I want to learn more about Artificial Intelligence and its implication on business strategy and enrolled in one of the MIT "Executive Certificates."

At MIT, each participant receives a certificate of completion for every course they successfully pass. But the school also offers three "Executive Certificates" in the subjects of management and leadership, strategy and innovation, as well as technology, operations, and value chain management.

"An Executive Certificate demonstrates the person's commitment to learning and development and the acquisition of new skills and leadership capabilities,"[91] says Kate Anderson, senior director of MIT Sloan Executive Education.

Participants are eager to include their courses and certificates on their CVs and in their LinkedIn profiles, she says. MIT Sloan offers verified digital credentials that are encrypted with blockchain technology, which participants can also share via email.

Individuals are empowered with evidence of their capabilities, certifications, and achievements that are verified in real time, at the click of a button. Earners are bridging the divide between school and work, gaining recognition for skills developed on the job as well as in the classroom. To ensure validity, forgery-proof metadata built into the badge includes who earned it, who issued it and when, and if and when the credential expires.

Skills can become the coin of the realm in a knowledge economy. The translation of skills into digital credentials can unlock the potential of both individuals and organizations. In the near future, we may see more and more employers begin to move away from filtering applicants based largely

---

91 "Executive Education: Why Certificates & Credentials Are Becoming More Popular | Businessbecause". 2019. Businessbecause.Com.

on where they went to school and to an approach where they evaluate the actual competencies prospective employees possess to determine if there is a match.

By providing a digital, information-rich record of work place relevant skills and competencies, attributed to an individual. These alternative forms of verification will create a new and dynamic ecosystem for the evaluation of applied learning in the workplace, which will disrupt higher education's traditional advantage and allow non-higher education institutions to be active in the credentialing process.

Certificates and credentials also appear to mean something to recruiters: three quarters of 600 employers surveyed by FutureLearn, an online learning platform, said that proof of completing online programs would help them decide whether or not to promote an employee. The same number of companies said such courses could differentiate mid-level managers in the recruitment process.[92]

Richard Garrett, chief research officer at Eduventures, has poured cold water on the prospect of alternative credentials replacing degrees anytime soon, but added "if they did, it could help tackle higher education's cost challenges."

---

92 *Ibid*

The challenge for all innovation in this area is that the "Job" that human resource professionals are hiring the college degree to do is efficiently disqualify a large portion of applicants, so they can focus on a smaller number of high potential candidates. At this point, no new solution competes with the efficiency of glancing at a resume to see where someone went to college. As a result, many emerging alternative credentials have served as supplements to and differentiators on top of the degree, but not full replacements.

A CLOSER RELATIONSHIP BETWEEN
EMPLOYERS AND UNIVERSITIES

LinkedIn Learning's Insider Survey gathered information from a panel of thirty to forty-five notable learning and development experts, including corporate learning executives, leaders from educational nonprofits, and industry analysts focused on enterprise training and development.[93]

The big headline is that 60 percent of Insiders believe that more employers will move to skills-based hiring by choosing candidates based on what they can do, rather than their degree or pedigree. Assessments that objectively *suss* out one's skills are on the rise, said one Insider.

---

93 *"2019 Workplace Learning Report". 2019. Learning.Linkedin.Com.*

At the same time, 57 percent of Insiders said employers will place more value on nontraditional credentials—and that those seeking jobs should seriously consider them as a way to build their profile. Although this could move in concert with a shift beyond focusing on degree, in practice in 2017, this will more likely be a continuation of the trend toward candidates gathering additional credentials beyond the degree through boot camps and the like.

In support of this trend, start-ups are now also emerging, such as *Guild Education*, which help create and support relationships between employers and universities. What is interesting is that although direct relationships between employers and universities attract headlines, they are complex to structure and difficult to manage. That creates a question as to how scalable they will be. The rise of intermediary organizations with the express purpose of managing these relationships signals that the education as a benefit trend could be more enduring.

What's interesting given the projected education as a benefit trend is that many have noted that the skills gap is not entirely caused by educational organizations inadequately preparing students for today's jobs, but also by employers retreating from investing enough in the training of new employees. To combat this, 71 percent predict that partnering with outside training providers will be the best strategy to get ahead of the widening skills gap. Many people believe companies should take a multi-pronged approach that combines formal, informal, and social learning.

To facilitate this, according to Insiders, *Microlearning*—content delivered in small, specific segments—as well as *On-Demand Learning*—content accessible at any time, from any device—will see the most growth among learning technologies in the next years.

HOW LINKEDIN IS CONNECTING LEARNING WITH EMPLOYMENT

LinkedIn has launched a new site called LinkedIn Learning, an e-learning portal tailored to individuals, but also catering to businesses looking to keep training their employees, and beyond that even relevant for educational institutions who are looking to explore e-learning courses. LinkedIn's CEO, Jeff Weiner, described the education has "one of our most important priorities." [94]LinkedIn also sees education as a business opportunity, with "just in time" experience training from LinkedIn as a key way of meeting that demand.

Entering the education and learning world makes a lot of sense for the company, with the amount of data LinkedIn

---

94 *"Linkedin Doubles Down On Education With Linkedin Learning, Updates Desktop Site – Techcrunch". 2019.*

has been collecting on their users, now they have opportunity to leverage the data and offer their users to learn new skills based on jobs that they are interested in.

To support this, LinkedIn recently announced the $1.5 billion acquisition of online education company Lynda.com. Lynda.com provides video courses to paying subscribers hoping to learn online, with tutorials on a wide range of business subjects from Web design to 3-D animation. What LinkedIn is doing is simply copying the education service and meshing it with its data. The service will also show users aggregate info about people who have taken the course, their job titles and other skills, so users can be better informed about the steps to take after completing their training.

LinkedIn is painting a scenario in which people search for a job, see the skills required for that job, and then are directed to a course from Lynda.com that will train them in those skills. Alternatively, a recruiter could search for available candidates based on the courses they've taken.

According to Tanya Staples, the VP of Learning Content at LinkedIn, "LinkedIn Learning platform, has the highest engagement numbers in the industry". "What's the special sauce? We leverage data from nearly 600M member profiles and billions of interactions to automatically deliver personalized course recommendations that quickly connect learners to the most relevant, applicable learning." "Our new 2019 Workplace Learning Report shows that understanding skills gaps is a top concern for talent leaders and we don't see that changing for the foreseeable future."[95]

How is LinkedIn helping companies become learning organizations specifically with regards to the impact of artificial intelligence and automation on their workforce?

"Too often, the narrative around AI and automation is driven by a fear that robots will take our jobs. While it's certainly true that the nature of work is changing, and some industries will be impacted more than others, we'll still need humans to do the work that robots can't do like managing people or strategic decision-making. We've found that the biggest skills gaps in the workforce today are also ones that automation can't replace—soft skills such as communication, team-building, or leadership skills."

"Given the rapid pace of change these days, continuously learning is an imperative that can put both employees and businesses at risk of becoming obsolete. And, we see plenty of signs in the market—and our own business—that the 'lifelong learning' switch has turned on."

---

95 *"2019 Workplace Learning Report". 2019. Learning.Linkedin.Com.*

A new ATD survey said that 45% of talent development leaders believe lifelong learning is a top priority, and 55% of high-performing organizations in the report actively encouraged lifelong learning. The real key to lifelong learning is making sure that anyone who wants to learn has access to learning opportunities and that the online solutions are not only easy-to-use, but also quickly connects them to relevant, applicable content.[96]

The rapid pace of technology change and the shrinking shelf life of skills means that an incumbent workforce increasingly needs ongoing training and development to meet the changing needs of business.

"Our recent research among L&D leaders also suggest that L&D budgets are expected to continue to grow, despite looming predictions of a market downturn." "When workers up-skill their soft skills or gain credentials, they're making long-term career investments, they're equipped to do excellent work and are often happier at work. The job stability that they can get from developing their interpersonal skills could last for several years, potentially outlasting an economic downturn."

"For employers, up-skilling is an especially important tool for addressing economic uncertainty when considering how

---

96 *"The Future Of Linkedin Learning And The Link Between Education And Work". 2019. Forbes.Com.*

automation and AI continue replacing jobs at a rapid pace." [97]Says Staples.

THE FUTURE OF ORGANIZATIONAL LEARNING

The primary challenge facing today's C-suite is the management, growth, and development of the organization's most important asset, its people. Failure or success in these areas directly correlates with how well and to what extent they provide employees with proper training, skills, and leadership development.

The "one size fits all" learning programs may have worked years ago when employees often held static positions, but in today's knowledge-based economy that is no longer the case. The speed of change, and the failure of organizations to evolve their training programs to be more agile and adaptive, has created an ever-widening gap between employee learning needs and the organization's ability to meet them.

Adaptive enterprises win by identifying future opportunities and proactively reconfiguring themselves, including their business models, in the face of changing customer and market demands. To become an adaptive enterprise requires significant investments in technology

---

97 *ibid*

transformation, in culture building, and in setting up structures and processes. For example, an adaptive enterprise must be able to alter its business concept based on insights that improve the company's odds of fulfilling future customer demand.

According to Forrester, as customers raise the bar on their demands—and shift their preferences more frequently—organizations must build a delivery organization that's adaptive, too. This new adaptive workforce taps into technology innovations, particularly AI and automation, to become more flexible, responsive, and productive and to support the broader adaptive enterprise strategy.[98]

THE ADAPTIVE WORKFORCE HAS THREE KEY CHARACTERISTICS:

- *Burstable.* Adaptive workforces can flex up or down their resources in response to changing conditions by tapping into next generation labor pools: the talent economy (contingent workforce providers, the gig economy, or employees from the partner ecosystem) and the automation economy (AI, business process management, robotic process automation, and other intelligent software that can complete tasks).

---

98 *"The Future Of Work Is An Adaptive Workforce".* 2019. Forbes.Com.

- *Less hierarchical.* Traditional corporate organizations are extremely vertical and siloed: An employee starts working in one organizational function and continues to do so throughout their entire career at the firm. Now, a "botmaster" who manages bots in the finance department can move to do similar work in HR, contributing and also learning new skills in the process.

- *Composable.* Swarm teams, which assemble employees from cross-functional groups to destroy silos, drive innovation, and solve problems, exemplify the adaptive workforce. They can be assembled and disassembled as projects complete or as conditions evolve.

HERE'S HOW BUSINESSES CAN STOP WASTING BILLIONS ON FAILED LEARNING INITIATIVES

Gartner found that 70 percent of employees say they have not mastered the skills they need to do their jobs today, while 80 percent said they lack both the skills for their current role and those they need for their future career.[99]

So, where are workers turning instead for guidance or recommendations when they need to learn something for their jobs

---

99 *"Gartner Says Only 20 Percent Of Employees Have The Skills Needed For Both Their Current Role And Their Future Career".* 2019. Gartner.

or careers? Sixty-five percent go to websites and 62 percent turn to their professional networks. Just over half (53 percent) go to search engines.

There is a crucial role for learning platforms inside businesses. It's up to them to show employees the kinds of skills the business needs and expects to need in the future. It's up to companies to create and encourage knowledge sharing, allow employees to guide each other to the best content on any given subject, and help employees discover internal experts who can help them learn new skills. The best learning platforms also allow employees to create their own learning content, such as training videos, that other employees can access on their own time.

Most importantly, businesses need to build and embrace cultures of continuous learning. A commitment to learning should be communicated from the very top in the C-suite and supported by managers, who make sure their employees have time to learn as part of the normal work week.

DEBRIEFING BASED LEARNING MODEL

Another effective way for organization to learn is through Debriefing. Debriefing is known by many names. In the U.S. Army it is called the after-action review or AAR. In business it often goes by the unfortunate name of postmortem. In psychology and military aviation, however, it is known as a *Debrief.*

"We know that debriefing works; that it is a powerful continuous performance improvement tool."

Recently, Scott Tannenbaum and Christopher Cerasoli conducted a meta-analysis of forty-six separate studies of debriefing in which they discovered that debriefing increased performance by an average of 25 percent.[100]

So, if debriefing is so effective, why doesn't everyone do it? It isn't that debriefing is difficult to do, or that it takes too much time, or even that it is costly in resources.

Tannenbaum and Cerasoli's study cites that debriefing is both cheap and easy. The reason debriefing isn't practiced more often in organizations is that leaders simply don't know how to do it and those that try their hand at it don't have the simple structure and basic training to capitalize on its full value.

We live in a world where we are 95 percent of the time in the performance zone versus 5 percent of the time in the Learning Zone. In most companies the management routines

---

100 *CP, Tannenbaum. 2019. "Do Team And Individual Debriefs Enhance Performance? A Meta-Analysis.*

don't involve time for learning and tools to share knowledge which leads to inefficiency.

LEARNING TO DEBRIEF LIKE THE ISRAEL AIR FORCE

The Israeli Air Force (IAF) is based on a culture of continues learning and personal debriefing.

This culture led the IAF to be one of the best in the world, and train its pilot to the highest levels, in only half of the average time. But there's no reason why learning the IAF way can't be used in business.

How does this work in the Israeli Air Force?

First of all, every event is debriefed. It doesn't matter the size or severity of the event: each and every IAF activity, each and every maneuver, in training or combat – is debriefed in the same manner.

Every flight will start with a briefing and will end with a debriefing for the flight crew.

Every squadron has an officer responsible for documenting all the lessons, and a system to document the knowledge gained and distribute it to whoever needs to see it.

This process plays a critical role in the IAF's method of handling an always changing environment in a very tough neighborhood. Very similar to a growth company, the IAF cannot afford not to learn its lessons on the move.

The debriefing culture in the IAF, prizes personal responsibility and openness. Sharing the conclusions of a debriefing session is hardly regarded as humiliating or as something that would come back to haunt a soldier. Imagine a room with one hundred pilots that sit together and talk about their mistakes. It's not unusual to see the youngest pilot talk about his mistakes, and then the commander shares his mistakes with everyone. [101]

What makes the IAF debrief such an effective tool?

The IAF debriefing method uses the facts rather than feelings, and helps wrap those in a comprehensive, easy-to-use way by asking 3 simple questions:

What Happened? Facts only.

Why Did It Happen? The reasons.

---

101 *"How Debriefing Like The Israeli Air Force Can Help Your Business".* 2019. Forbes.Com.

What should I (or we) do different next time? Creating a practical "to do" list to improve or change, which could be applied to others as well.

But following these 3 questions is not enough. There needs to be a genuine interest in improvement, and a culture that supports an open conversation.

In practice, the IAF manages to create an environment where people can speak freely. That is done by using several principles:

1. *Resist and obey.* If you see something wrong, you have to say it is wrong, why it is wrong, and what should be done to fix it. if the outcome of the conversation is not what you expected you still need to obey and behave accordingly.

2. *Don't judge the person – judge the situation, it might be you next time.* The conversation should be around the facts and what might have been done differently, and not about the person doing the drill.

3. *If you don't do – then you won't make any mistakes.* If a young officer encounters a problem, or sees a problem that needs to be fixed, it is expected from him/her to come up with a solution. It might not be the best solution,

but they will have to come up with one nonetheless. That principle teaches people within the IAF to take responsibility and to move the organization forward.

Brutally honest criticism, the kind that is found in elite military units, is hardly found in the business world, despite the fact that it is one of the most beneficial practices any organization can adopt.

* * *

Organizations today are faced with overwhelming, rapid change, which can impact every aspect of business. Along with this, there are up to four generations of people working side-by-side, making today's organizations more diverse. In order to survive in the current business atmosphere organizations must be more innovative regarding workforce learning. Replacing the learning practices of the Machine Age with models reflective of the 21st Century is an important initiative for the future of organizational learning.

Learning in today's work environment is continuous due to the increased data flow and changes affecting the workplace. Staying on top of required skills and knowledge is all about learning, unlearning, and relearning

CHAPTER 8

HOW TO SUCCEED IN THE FUTURE OF WORK

———

- The Single Most Important Skill of the Twenty-First Century

- Why Even New Grads Need to Reskill for the Future

- How to Develop Your Own LLL Strategy

- Five Career Tips for College Students

- Final Words—The Future Is up to You

THE SINGLE MOST IMPORTANT SKILL
OF THE TWENTY-FIRST CENTURY

"The illiterate of the 21st century will not be those who cannot read and write, but those who cannot learn, unlearn and relearn."

— ALVIN TOFFLER

The workplace is changing rapidly and becoming a knowledge-based world. Your collective knowledge about yourself and your industry are the key to your future. As time passes, it becomes even more apparent that knowledge begets knowledge, and new competencies drive careers forward.

The single most important skill of the twenty-first century is: *Learnability*; the desire and capability to develop in-demand skills.

When was the last time you read something from an unusual perspective in your industry?

When have you taken the time to wrap your head around a new industry?

Change is the only thing that is constant in today's workplace. To keep up, you need to keep learning. Learning drives adaptability. Most people know this, but it's often easier said than done. Between deadlines, meetings, family life, and everything else in between, there isn't much time for a career-boosting class, but you can change that. As long as you are ready to take responsibility for your career. No matter where you are on the career ladder, it's important to continue learning and develop new skills. It's the only way to survive in the twenty-first century.

Learning helps you become more open to change. When people embrace lifelong learning, it becomes another part of their career journey. A learning mind-set makes it less likely you'll be thrown off when a project changes, your employer changes growth strategy, or when a job function undergoes transformation.

While others scramble to figure out where to go from here, lifelong learners maintain momentum and productivity even in the face of radical change at work.

WHY EVEN NEW GRADS NEED TO RESKILL FOR THE FUTURE

College degree programs simply cannot keep pace with how fast things are changing in the workforce.

It means that new grads need to be better prepared for what lies ahead. Reskilling and continuously building skills throughout a career are important to bring about lateral (and indeed vertical) career transitions for all ages but will be particularly vital for new grads as they strive to keep up with the skills and work of the future.[102]

WHAT SHOULD NEW GRADS BE DOING?

Think about the skills that you have now and the job you want 18 months from now, and then:

- *Identify the key soft skills you have and need.* You can then see where you have gaps and put learning goals in place to fill them. Examples of important power skills include critical thinking, problem-solving, communication, and learning agility.

- *Consider core technical skills you have that are likely to stay in high demand.* Such as digital literacy, data science, and data analytics. And then build upon those skills.

- *Focus on skills that are portable and that will be critical regardless of what field you enter.* Highlighting your transferable skills will showcase your abilities in unique ways. For example, the data analytics skills you developed in your marketing job may be just as

---

102 *"How New Grads Can Develop The Skills They Didn'T Learn In College". 2019. Harvard Business Review.*

valuable — or even more valuable — in e-commerce or product development.

- *Keep a permanent, personal list of past and future learning.* This will help you have better conversations about your skills in interviews and on the job.

- *Discover, filter, and apply your learning.* There are many resources available at low or no cost. Utilize technology.

- *Be prepared to be thrust into decision-making responsibilities from day one.* Practice more self-direction, in work and in learning. You may be fortunate enough to have a manager or a mentor who can help guide you, but ultimately only you are responsible for your own career.

HOW TO DEVELOP YOUR OWN LLL STRATEGY

1. SHORT-TERM AND LONG-TERM LEARNING GOALS

Think about the skills and knowledge you need to stay current now and prepare for the future. You don't have to learn every skill at once, but you owe it to yourself to be the best you can be. To be an effective learner, any skill you choose to learn should fit into the bigger picture of your life and work—your career path.

2. LEARNING CAN HELP YOU MEET IMMEDIATE OR FUTURE NEEDS

If you intend to improve your skills in the next three or six months, you can get feedback from your employer about your skills that may need upgrading. Other clues like tasks you tend to avoid or struggle with because of knowledge or skills you don't have can help you choose what to focus on now or in the future. You can also focus on the big picture, define your career path and choose the skills you need to get to your ultimate career goal.

3. KNOW YOUR LEARNING STYLE

Do you learn best on your own or in a group? Do you prefer audio, video or a combination of both?

Are you a hands-on learner?

Depending on your current circumstances, you can pick the opportunities that suit your learning style including hands-on workshops, or video-based course if your learning style is visual.

In the abundance-based economy of online learning, opportunities are endless. You can learn on your own, at work, from mentors or role models.

You can also learn online following blogs, downloading podcasts, taking a class, and so on. Or through magazines, journals, seminars, videos, and broadcasts. And you can also learn by attending classes at an educational institution, in person or online.

FIVE CAREER TIPS FOR COLLEGE STUDENTS

College is important educationally and culturally, but what you already understand and what you learn at university alone doesn't equip you for today's job market.

It's important to get practical work experience early. Do everything you can to improve your knowledge of the applied side of the field. Gain practical experience (the more the merrier) while you're in school. Show employers how what you learned in class can solve a real-world business problem. For example, start with data visualizations, and then combine this with telling a story via blog post. Build a real product and find even one customer to pay you for it. Combine tangible work experience along with your education. Everyone has a college degree these days. How will you differentiate?

Here are five more career tips to a successful career launch:

1. LEARNABILITY IS THE PATH TO CAREER SECURITY

In an environment where new skills emerge as fast as others become extinct, employability is less about what you already know and more about your capacity to learn. By focusing on learnability—the desire and ability to adapt your skills to remain employable—millennials are redefining career security.

Ninety-three percent want ongoing skills development and four out of five say the opportunity to learn a new skill is a top factor when considering a new job. Employers would do well to listen up and consider how they create a learning culture that motivates and retains millennials, because what works for them works for the rest of the workforce, too.

2. YOU GOT THE LICENSE TO BE CREATIVE—USE IT!

There's a difference between being creative to being innovative, according to Gavin Suss, creativeness is something that you're born with and can work on, just like a muscle. Innovation is something that comes as a result to creative thinking, so essentially by being more creative you're also become more innovative.

3. EMBRACE DISRUPTION AND TAKE ADVANTAGE OF TECHNOLOGY

It's no secret that the job-for-life model no longer exists— but amazing that 65 percent of students starting their first year of school this year will eventually do jobs that don't yet exist. So, without a doubt today's and tomorrow's workforce will need to keep reskilling to stay relevant through longer working lives.

Some jobs will be significantly impacted by automation and robotics, and new jobs will be created in ways that are hard to predict, but what we know for sure is that the ability to adapt and learn will be a skill that will provide employment security for many as the environment changes.

4. FIND OUT WHAT YOU CARE ABOUT AND TRY TO ALIGN IT WITH YOUR WORK

It might sound clichéd and it's not always possible, but it's important to be interested—even passionate—about what you do. In this respect, the millennial generation is doing a good job. They/We care—about communities, about giving back—and they look for that in their employers too.

Eight in ten millennials in Mexico, India, and Brazil say working for employers who are socially responsible and aligned to their values is important. A majority of millennials everywhere say purpose is a priority. Almost half of Generation Z go as far as saying that in choosing a job, working for a company that helps make the world a better place would be as important as the salary.

5. TIE LEARNING DIRECTLY TO IN-DEMAND CAREERS

You need to start spending time preparing for the future even when there are more important things to do in the present and even when there is no immediately apparent return to your efforts.

FINAL WORDS

THE FUTURE IS UP TO YOU

———

The future is yours to shape. You have the power to change and adapt your skills to stay relevant and indispensable. You need to start spending time preparing for the future even when there are more important things to do in the present and even when there is no immediately apparent return to your efforts. If you find yourself trapped for the foreseeable future because you are stuck in a soul-crushing job, remember, you always have two obvious options: settle or plan for a career change.

Don't be afraid of the unknown if you decide to pursue your life's work, because everything is unknown.

Most people can't show their most amazing work to the rest of us because they fear criticisms. They feel inadequate. They are scared people will think it's not good enough. Others are living in their comfort zones because of fear. But remember everything great happens outside your safe zone.

Choose to reinvent you career and make the most of the exciting, and promising future of work.

If you're not sure what you want to do next, yet you know you want a change, you should go ahead and get started, with a focus on strengthening your core skills.

It is important also to adopt a growth mind-set. Be prepared for lifelong learning, that is, to continuously unlearn old skills, and relearn new ones. In particular, you should focus on skills that are likely to be in high demand in the next ten years.

If you really want to have a meaningful career, you have to feel part of something bigger than yourself. You need to feel a sense of purpose. Look for it and do it. If you pursue your dreams long enough, compounding takes effect. Momentum will surge.

Enjoy your journey, and Good Luck!

APPENDIX

INTRODUCTION

Christopher Ingraham, "7 ways $1.6 trillion in student loan debt affects the U.S. economy", The   Washington Post, June 25, 2019

Henry-Nickie, Makada. 2019. "AI Should Worry Skilled Knowledge Workers Too". Brookings

"Jobs Lost, Jobs Gained: What The Future Of Work Will Mean For Jobs, Skills, And Wages". 2019. Mckinsey & Company.

Jordan Valinsky, CNN Business. 2019. "Amazon Plans To Retrain 100,000 Employees". CNN.

"Self-Driving Cars Will Take Over By 2040". 2019. Forbes.Com.

"Want To Be A Federal Cyber Pro? This Program Will Train You". 2019. Govloop.

CHAPTER ONE: THE FUTURE OF WORK IN THE DIGITAL AGE

"Disruptive Technologies And Their Impact On The Future Of Work". 2019.

"Employment Trends". 2019. The Future Of Jobs.

"From Employee Experience To Human Experience: Putting Meaning Back Into Work". 2019.

Georgette Yakman, "Developing STEAM Education To Improve Students' Innovative Ability | STEAM Education". 2019. STEAM Education.

John Hagel, Jeff Schwartz, and Josh Bersin, "Navigating The Future Of Work". 2019

Klaus Schwab, The Fourth Industrial Revolution, January 3,

"Preparing Tomorrow'S Workforce For The Fourth Industrial Revolution". 2019.

"The Fourth Industrial Revolution | Special Feature". 2019. Encyclopedia Britannica.

"The Fourth Industrial Revolution: What It Means And How To Respond". 2019. World Economic Forum.

"The Future Of Work Is Creative, Flexible, And Human". 2019. Medium.

"The New Tech Talent You Need To Succeed In Digital". 2019. Mckinsey & Company.

"The SHL Talent Report". 2019. Lessaccent.Com.

CHAPTER TWO: THE SYMBIOTIC WORKFORCE OF THE FUTURE

"A Machine May Not Take Your Job, But One Could Become Your Boss". 2019. Nytimes.Com.

Clifford, Catherine. 2019. "Google CEO: A.I. Is More Important Than Fire Or Electricity".

"Employment Trends". 2019. The Future Of Jobs.

"Future of jobs in India" 2019. Ey.Com.

"Gartner Says AI Augmentation Will Create $2.9 Trillion Of Business Value In 2021". 2019. Gartner

"Gartner Says By 2020, Artificial Intelligence Will Create More Jobs Than It Eliminates". 2019. Gartner.

"How Humans And AI Are Working Together In 1,500 Companies". 2019. Harvard Business Review.

"JOBS LOST, JOBS GAINED: WORKFORCE TRANSITIONS IN A TIME OF AUTOMATION". 2019. Mckinsey.Com.

Kshirsagar, Alap, Bnaya Dreyfuss, Guy Ishai, Ori Heffetz, and Guy Hoffman. 2019. "Monetary-Incentive Competition Between Humans And Robots: Experimental Results".

"New Robots, New Jobs". 2019. US Day One Blog.

"Robot Density Rises Globally". 2019. IFR International Federation Of Robotics

Services, Products, Market-specific Solutions, Topic Areas, Jobs Careers

"The Deloitte 2019 Global Human Capital Trends - 2019.

"The Future Of Jobs Report 2018". 2019. World Economic Forum.

"The History Of Artificial Intelligence - Science In The News". 2019. Science In The News.

"These Countries Have The Most Robot Workers". 2019. World Economic Forum.

Useem, Jerry. 2019. "At Work, Expertise Is Falling Out Of Favor".

"Where Machines Could Replace Humans--And Where They Can'T (Yet)". 2019. Mckinsey & Company.

Chapter Three: New Skills for New Economies

Center, Microsoft. 2019. "Microsoft And General Assembly Launch Partnership To Close The Global AI Skills Gap - Stories".

"Council Post: Here's Why We Need To Democratize Artificial Intelligence". 2019. Forbes.Com.

"How Can We Best Prepare For Job Automation?". 2019. Medium.

"Linkedin Surveyed 5,000 Talent Professionals And Found The Top 3 Ways Employers Are Screening For Soft Skills". 2019. Inc.Com.

"Machines Will Do More Tasks Than Humans By 2025 But Robot Revolution Will Still Create 58

Million Net New Jobs In Next Five Years". 2019. World Economic Forum.s

Million Net New Jobs In Next Five Years". 2019. World Economic Forum.

"Retraining And Reskilling Workers In The Age Of Automation". 2019. Mckinsey & Company.

"Tech Giants Are Paying Huge Salaries For Scarce A.I. Talent". 2019. Nytimes.Com.

"Tencent Says There Are Only 300,000 AI Engineers Worldwide, But Millions Are Needed". 2019. The Verge.

"The Jobs Of The Future – And Two Skills You Need To Get Them". 2019. World Economic Forum.

Chapter Four - The Disruption in Higher Education

"Chapter 1: The Future Of Jobs And Skills". 2019. The Future Of Jobs.

Christensen, Clayton M, and Henry J Eyring. The Innovative University : Changing the DNA of Higher Education from the inside Out. San Francisco, Jossey-Bass, 2011.=

"Class Of 2030 | | Microsoft EDU". 2019. Educationblog.Microsoft.Com.

Hess, Abigail. 2019. "Harvard Business School Professor: Half Of American Colleges Will Be Bankrupt In 10 To 15 Years". CNBC.

Holm, Erik. 2019. "August Jobs Report: Everything You Need To Know". WSJ

Loans". 2019. Federal Student Aid.

Lucy Sherriff, ernst-and-young-removes-degree-classification-entry-criteria, Huffingtonpost.Co.Uk. 2019.

Mitchell, Josh. 2019. "The Long Road To The Student Debt Crisis". WSJ.

"Student Debt And The Class Of 2017 - The Institute For College Access & Success". 2019. The Institute For College Access & Success.

Stephens, Dale. 2019. "A Smart Investor Would Skip The M.B.A.". WSJ.

"Student Loan Debt Statistics In 2019: A $1.5 Trillion Crisis". 2019. Forbes.Com.

"Student Debt Rising Worldwide | Yaleglobal Online". 2019. Yaleglobal.Yale.Edu.

"The Best-Performing Ceos In The World 2018". 2019. Harvard Business Review.

"The Future Of Work Won't Be About College Degrees, It Will Be About Job Skills". 2019. CNBC.

CHAPTER FIVE - THE PATH TO TRANSFORMATION IN EDUCATION

"Coding Bootcamps: A Glimpse At The Future Of Education?". 2019. Medium.

"Education Should Be Like Everything Else. An On-Demand Service". 2019. World Economic Forum.

"Exploring New Routes To Success - Kaplan". 2019. Kaplan.

"This Will Be The Biggest Disruption In Higher Education". 2019. Forbes.Com.

"Udemy Thinks It's Cracked The Future Of Online Education". 2019. Time

"What Will Higher Education Look Like 5, 10 Or 20 Years From Now?". 2019. Goodcall.Com.

CHAPTER SIX - THE PATH TO TRANSFORMATION IN EDUCATION

Hill, David. 2019. "AI Teaching Assistant Helped Students Online—And No One Knew The Difference". Singularity Hub.

"The Autonomous Learner Model For Developing Potential". 2019. Uncw.Edu.

"What Is Personalized Learning?". 2019. Medium.

CHAPTER SEVEN: TIME FOR A NEW RELATIONSHIP BETWEEN LEARNING AND WORK

CP, Tannenbaum. 2019. "Do Team And Individual Debriefs Enhance Performance? A Meta-Analysis.

"Deloitte Millennial Survey". 2019.

"Executive Education: Why Certificates & Credentials Are Becoming More Popular | Businessbecause". 2019. Businessbecause.Com.

"Gartner Says Only 20 Percent Of Employees Have The Skills Needed For Both Their Current Role And Their Future Career". 2019. Gartner.

"How Debriefing Like The Israeli Air Force Can Help Your Business". 2019. Forbes.Com.

"Linkedin Doubles Down On Education With Linkedin Learning, Updates Desktop Site – Techcrunch". 2019.

"Skills, Not Job Titles, Are The New Metric For The Labour Market". 2019. World Economic Forum.

"The Future Of Linkedin Learning And The Link Between Education And Work". 2019. Forbes.Com.

"The Future Of Work Is An Adaptive Workforce". 2019. Forbes.Com.

"Universities Should Be Preparing Students For The Gig Economy". 2019. Harvard Business Review.

"Workplace Learning Report". 2019. Learning.Linkedin.Com.

Chapter Eight: How to Succeed in the Future of Work

"How New Grads Can Develop The Skills They Didn'T Learn In College". 2019. Harvard Business Review.

BOOK ACKNOWLEDGEMENTS

———

First and foremost, I'd like to thank my family — my beautiful wife Alona Cohen and my little princess Netta Cohen for their love and constant support.

To my mother Dalia Cohen and my father Shimon Cohen, thank you for believing in me after all the things I put you through during my childhood. And to my sisters Reut and Chan Cohen for helping me promote my pre-launch campaign.

Thank you to all my interviewees for taking the time out of your very busy schedule to share with me your deep and very insightful knowledge.

Thank you to my Georgetown friends for sharing with me your valuable feedback from my first thoughts about the topic of the book all the way to my final manuscript.

Thank you to my high school friends Niv Biton and Tomer Kogman for your huge support in my Crowdfunding campaign and for rooting for me on social media.

And thank you to everyone who pre-ordered the eBook, paperback, and multiple copies to make publishing possible, helped spread the word about Working with Robots to gather amazing momentum, and helped me publish a book I am proud of. I am sincerely grateful for all your help.

Lastly, a HUGE thank you to New Degree Press, especially Eric Koster for actually thinking that I can write a book and become an author, and for Brian Bies and Cynthia Tucker for supporting me throughout this incredible journey of making this dream a reality.